Surviving Myself

Jay Eddy

Jay Eddy

ISBN: 979-8-9893253-1-3

Dedication

This book is dedicated to the following people who have made their way into my heart for the following reasons:

Vicki for her shyness, Marit for her friendship, David for his wisdom, Kathy for her shared tenderness, Lori and Lisa for their touch, Wayne and Charles for their laughter, Rosie for her sweetness and acceptance, Sandy and Jerry for their generosity, Debbie for my children, Teren and Ethan for their forgiveness, Dad for his strength, Mom for her unwavering love, Karen for sharing the front seat, and John for the ride home. Thank you.

Acknowledgment

I would like to acknowledge Steve Hegna for his steadfast faith and encouragement for me to continue writing and complete this work. He brought back my enthusiasm and validated the expression of my experience. I would also like to acknowledge the men of our Tuesday night men's group who were willing to read the manuscript and offer insight. I trust them deeply with my testimony. I want to acknowledge my best friend John Gaier, with whom I have shared so much of my life, for his affirmation of my character and genuine excitement for the publication of Surviving Myself. Finally, I want to acknowledge the author Michael Perry who was willing to take time to answer my email about writing and publishing. He shared some sage advice that convinced me to take the final step. I am honored to acknowledge each of you. God Bless!

Table Of Contents

About the Author

Jay Eddy is a 64-year-old semi-retired senior who will be celebrating his 25th wedding anniversary to his second wife Kathy this year. Together they raised five children, Jay's 2, and Kathy's 3, and enjoy 7 grandchildren from the group. Jay works part-time as a manager for a senior living cooperative and has spent the last 8 years as Mayor of Black River Falls, WI . Jay considers himself "born again" and he participates in multiple faith study groups encouraging a personal relationship with God. He strives to live the mission of Loving God, Loving People and serving Our World.

Preface

I wanted to write to the men who shared my experience of being a baby boomer growing up in the 60's and 70's. Little did I know we would be the last participants of the traditional American family which had existed since the end of World War II.

Our parents had survived the Great Depression and the War and like every generation were products of the way they were raised. The father was the head of the house and enjoyed the trappings of being the king. He gave orders that were to be carried out by his servants which were his wife and children. Everyone was subject to his demands and he alone was allowed to express every emotion he experienced. That emotion was anger more often than not. Children were to be seen and not heard. They also had better acknowledge his reign or be subject to his punishment/discipline which in those days included physical reprimands with a belt, paddle, slap, hair pull, or other pain inducing action.

Mother's had little influence so they were relegated to being cook, maid, secretary, nurse, and protector when needed. With many families having 5 to 10 children a mother's job was never ending. This was in direct contrast to what was being portrayed on television at the time. Father Knows Best with Robert Young as Jim Anderson and Leave it to Beaver with Hugh Beaumont as Ward Cleaver showed a calm understanding fathers who consulted their wives and together, they would speak to their children with loving concern. They would point out the errors of their child's thinking and then offer some wise advice that would lead to a solution to the problem. By the end of the show the problem was solved and the family smiled in unison.

In contrast, the evening news revealed what was really happening in the world from daily counts of numbers of Americans killed in Vietnam to the riots on college campuses and in the south. We were left to learn about life experiences on our own. Our older siblings or friends ended up being the sources for information we sought on relationships, sex, music, smoking, drinking, or any of the other forbidden unspoken topics of the household.

We respected our fathers, loved our mothers, and understood that by the time we were 18 years old we had better go to college or have a job. Staying home was not an option. So with these things in mind, I made my way into the world and "Surviving Myself" is the story of how I did. I hope in some way that those who read this book and/or shared that same upbringing will relate to the experience and come away entertained, enlightened, or inspired.

Chapter One:

Fledgling Flirtations

Wendy sat across the aisle from me in Algebra 1. She had curly brown hair, big eyes, and a heartwarming smile. I could make her giggle until she blushed. Sometimes, she would laugh so hard that tears would form in her eyes, making them glisten. I found it extremely attractive, especially because she was shy, unlike most girls in the crowd I ran with. I was a class clown type. Some teachers thought of me as a smart ass. Upperclassmen called me a punk. "Egotistical" is the word my twin sister and her friends used to describe me. They didn't realize Wendy and I were both shy in the same way. I just had a more intense need to belong, so I developed my sense of humor to overcome that feeling.

I was a skinny, red-headed, freckle-faced sophomore—not the kind of guy on the cover of Teen Beat or that a girl pretends to kiss in her mirror. My best friend, Ryan, filled that role, and I was his trustworthy sidekick. Ryan was almost 6'4 and nearly 220 pounds. As a freshman, he had already been asked to play Varsity Football, Basketball, and Baseball. He was naturally big and worked hard to be the athlete he had become. He was living the dream of many high school boys. Although, some kids would make fun of his size and have given him the nickname "Ton Truck." The junior and senior boys had seen him as a threat to their territory. They would often test his toughness by harassing him or taking cheap shots at him on the field or in court. Even if it bothered him, he never let anyone know. If I saw that it bothered him, I wasn't telling. This began from the time we played Little League baseball together. He was the shortstop, and I played third. He was the biggest shortstop little league baseball had ever seen; he could stop anything. I had a great arm and a mastery of baseball chatter. We made a great pair. Who knew our friendship that began at eleven years old would last our entire lives?

Wendy and I continued our 7th-hour adolescent Algebra flirtations. She had begun to infiltrate my thoughts away from class and school. Maybe it was my time to explore the world of girlfriends like many classmates had already done. Often on Monday mornings, before class, a group of us boys would gather to spout stories about how their dates had gone over the weekend. Some would claim to have "scored" with this girl or that. We never knew if they were telling the truth, but we would listen intently, giggling at the details like children who heard a dirty word.

As winter faded into spring, it was time for the couple's event of the year. The prom was coming soon. Ryan had already asked his girlfriend, Ellen, and hoped I could land a date so we could double. Ellen and Ryan had been together since 8th grade. Ellen was a great friend of mine as well. She was a tall, statuesque blond with a great sense of humor. I found her to be a kind person with a soft spot in her heart for anyone or any animal we wouldn't have noticed. She and her girlfriends had visited the local animal shelter a few summers before and released all the dogs from their cages. Helping others came naturally to her; she would eventually make a career by teaching troubled kids. We had often gone out, just the three of us, and she would wait patiently while Ryan and I would be doing our boy things. I'm sure there were many times she hoped I would go home or find someone else to hang out with, but she knew I was a stray and needed attention too. Never having dated a girl in my life, I was very naïve and didn't know the girls were ahead of us boys and had more adult activities in mind. However, I got the message that prom would not be a threesome event. If I went with them, I had better find a date or stay home.

I had this really strong liking for Wendy, you know? Being in class with her was just so easy and comfortable. But then there's this whole idea of asking her to the prom, and I swear, it's like the scariest thing ever. I mean, what if she says no? I'd be totally crushed. It's like, maybe I should leave things as they are, you know? At least I spent one hour with her and the rest of the day with my thoughts about her. What if she said yes? I had no idea what to think then. I would be one of the guys then and maybe even have a story or two to share. I could say I had a girlfriend. Wow! My mother would be thrilled. So, I summoned my courage, and after class one day, I asked Wendy to go to the prom. She was so surprised that someone like me would want to go with her. In her eyes, I was part of the "It crowd." why would anyone ask a girl who was not a part of not-that group? I had never considered myself part of any crowd, not to mention the so-called "It crowd."

After lots of silly jokes and reassurance that I was serious about asking her out, she agreed. I was on cloud nine. I had taken the first step from junior high clown to regular high school boy. Little did I know where this journey would end.

My older brothers and sisters dated in high school but never went to prom. That meant our family was unfamiliar with all the preparations and hoopla surrounding such a big event. It turned out that I would need to buy a new suit, coat, and shoes. More importantly, I would have to know the color of Wendy's dress to buy a matched corsage. Before attending the dance, tradition dictated that we go out for supper at an upscale local restaurant. Suddenly, this quest for manhood would cost a substantial amount of money I didn't have. I did have a job washing dishes at the truck stop, but at $1.60 per hour, it would take months to cover these costs. Mom wanted me to go to the dance. If I was going, I should be dressed and expected to behave in a manner that reflected favorably upon our family. She convinced my father that they would cover this event's costs. I was thrilled and so thankful that my mother made this happen.

The plan was that Ryan would drive his mother's white Olds Toronado with a red interior. It was a beautiful car, unlike the Junkers most kids drove. He would pick up Ellen first, then me around 6 PM, and then we would go to Wendy's. We would have supper at the Rustic Mill. It was a local favorite, with great food and a pleasant ambiance. Wendy told me she would wear a purple dress, so I ordered a white corsage with purple-tipped petals. The plan was final; the big night couldn't get here fast enough.

The day of the prom finally arrived. I worked the morning shift at the truck stop so I could be home by 3 p.m. I then went to the flower shop, picked up Wendy's corsage, and headed home. After a small nap, I got into the shower around 4:30 PM. My dad teased me about not having to shave. My mom ironed my shirt and pants and put them on the bed. Once out of the shower, I combed my hair and went to my room to get dressed.

The phone rang, and my mom said it was for me. She said it was a girl's voice that she didn't recognize. It was Wendy, and she was crying. She said she was very sorry but couldn't go to the dance because she was sick. I was stunned and silent. My mother sensed something was wrong and asked me what was happening. I waved my hand at her as if to say, "Not right now, please." I told Wendy that it was ok and hoped she would get better. I hung up, went to my room quickly without saying anything to my parents, and closed the door. My eyes were filled with tears, and my head was spinning. What happened? Did I do something wrong? Was she really sick? How am I going to tell Ryan and Ellen? How am I going to face anybody at school? I guess the joke was on me this time, and, sure enough, I didn't find it funny.

My mom knocked on the door and asked if she could come in. She could see I was upset and wanted to know what had happened. When I told her, her eyes started to tear up, and I told her it was ok. Seeing my mother cry was the one thing I could never stand in my whole life. There was nothing my mom could do to make the situation better. I didn't want my dad to find out I was upset, so I told my mom to collect herself before telling him. My dad was a tough retired military man; according to him, crying was for babies, no matter the reason.

A half-hour passed, and all I did was sit on the edge of my bed in my underwear. All that planning and money we spent was for nothing. My mom came back to my room and said she had an idea. She asked, "Were there any other girls I could call to see if they want to go to the dance?" She was sure there must have been some girl who had not been asked who would like to go. Why waste the night sitting around feeling sad? At the very least, I could go to supper with everyone and see my other friends at the dance. There was a girl. I knew a little about her. I thought she was pretty, smart, and funny. Her name was Kristen; I gave her a call. It was a decision I would never regret.

Having raised four girls, I now have a greater appreciation for what a girl goes through to prepare for a big event like prom. It makes me wonder what went through Kristen's mind that night. I called her an hour before the date. She didn't know what to wear and wouldn't have had a chance to shop for that special prom dress like most other girls. There would be no time to call the salon and get her hair done. On top of all that, she would go with that goofy redhead who gets into trouble in class. Despite all that, she said yes. I was overjoyed. I was going to prom with a pretty girl, my best friend, and his girlfriend. Kristen saved me from what could have been the worst night of my life.

The truth behind Wendy's cancellation only became clear when she signed my senior yearbook. Various rumors were circulating among the other kids. Some claimed she went out drinking with different friends. In contrast, others insisted that they were there and mentioned she had been extremely ill, spending the day throwing up. She never communicated this to me; honestly, I didn't inquire either way.

She couldn't look at me in the 7th-hour algebra anymore. We didn't laugh together and never talked to each other again.

Finally, at the end of our senior year, when all the kids were exchanging their yearbooks to write farewell messages, I found out. Wendy wrote a long note, taking nearly three-quarters of one page. In her message, she apologized for not going with me that night. She said she was scared to go with me because she didn't think she was good enough for me. She hoped I would forgive her, and she was still very fond of me. She wished me luck for the future. What could I say? I never understood why she would think that. We might have had the time of our lives and maybe even more to follow.

Color My World was the theme of the prom. Ryan and Ellen picked me up and went to Kristen's house. I can remember knocking on the door and having her father answer. He was a Lutheran Minister, and it hadn't occurred to me until then that he might not favor his daughter going on a date. He was nice to me and invited me in. I waited by the door for Kristen so I could give her the corsage. Her dad was giving me the once-over while I waited. Her mother engaged me in pleasant conversation and complimented me on my chosen corsage. Kristen's mother was my 6th-grade music teacher. She was such a sweet person.

I don't think I have ever seen her without smiling. She was one of those people that seemed to like everyone, and everyone liked her. Kristen came into the room, and I gave her the corsage. She smiled and asked her mother to help her find something to pin it on with. After a few minutes of small talk, we were out the door and on our way to dinner and the dance. For all the tension and drama leading up to the prom, I can barely recall the dance itself. I only know we spent most of the night in conversation. Ryan and Ellen spent the night in each other's arms on the dance floor. Kristen and I spent the night getting to know one another. We watched other couples, commented on their clothes, looked at all the decorations, talked about our brothers and sisters, and became friends. I had forgotten about what had happened before the dance.

Surviving Myself

As the night ended, it was time to go. We jumped into the back seat of the Tornado and drove the 7 or 8 blocks to Kristen's house. Ellen and Ryan said their goodbyes as the car slowed, and Kristen thanked them for the evening. I was frozen in the back seat, not knowing what I should do at that point. I told her I had a wonderful time and thanked her for going with me. In my mind, I had decided that I should give her a kiss goodnight. She must have sensed that or could see something on my face because before I could lean over to deliver the goods, she had the door open and was leaving the car. Like a guy who had never kissed a girl, I lurched toward her, hoping to deliver a gentleman's kiss. She was nearly out of the car, so I barely touched her cheek. She went into the house, and the night was over.

Ryan and Ellen did well at not laughing at my clumsy and foolish attempt. They dropped me at home, and I walked into the house with what could be called a moral victory. I went on a date with a girl. No one died. The events of that night would have a lasting impression on me and guide my social life through the rest of high school.

I was so pumped for Monday to come around. I wanted to see Kristen again, find out what happened to Wendy, and see if my status as a class clown had changed in the eyes of the other kids. But I learned quickly in the boy's morning bull session that one date doesn't make anyone a Casanova. They had already heard about my failed kiss attempt. They hoped I would embellish the story with some of my usual self-deprecating humor. It went something like this, "Hey, did you hear? Eddy got a cheek." Note to self: don't try to be something you're not; don't ask someone to prom again. I made light of the failed kiss and went on my way. This experience effectively ended my formal high school dating career. What was I thinking? From now on, I will stay in my comfort zone. Dances would be out of the question, except for the lunchtime sock hop or the private gang parties held occasionally at someone's house. I didn't trust my judgment in the affairs of the heart.

Kristen and I would become best friends over the remainder of our high school years. We made each other laugh and shared our thoughts about the world, high school, teachers, and just about anything without hesitating or judging. I would get to know her family better and eventually attend the church where her father was pastor. I joined the choir that her mother directed and learned a great deal about faith. With her father's encouragement and guidance, I even decided to get baptized. Ryan and Ellen would serve as my Godparents for the ceremony.

Through numerous high school dances and special occasions like proms and winter carnivals, I watched as they came and went. Deep down, I wanted to ask Kristen to be my date, but I had learned a harsh lesson. I didn't want to mess up things with Kristen as I did with Wendy. Kristen would attend with other boys, and I would stay home. I was jealous and secretly and selfishly hoped she wouldn't have a good time with them. I was her boyfriend whether she knew it or not. But there was no way I would lose my relationship with this girl because I wanted more than just friendship. It was not easy. We would dance together at parties, swim, or bike ride during the summer. All it did was make her more attractive to me. My buddies often wondered why Kristen and I didn't date each other. It was apparent to them that I liked her and that she liked me. All I could hear was the old comment, "Eddy got a cheek." So yeah, never mind; I am good.

High school zipped by, and I enjoyed nearly every minute of it. By our senior year, I had made many friends and was elected class president as a write-in candidate. The class clown had become class president. My future looked bright. I still needed to overcome my fear of female rejection and attend the big dance. Until then, I would make plans to attend the "Prom Reject Party." Kids who hadn't been invited to the prom or had asked someone and got turned down participated in this party. Someone would usually host it at their house. We played games like Risk or Clue. We would have food and drinks and stay up late as if we were at the dance. They were fun parties that helped everyone overcome rejection for the big show. Misery loves company, and we decided we would be miserable together. It did help knowing there were just as many going as not.

Surviving Myself

I don't know what possessed me, but I decided that I would try again as prom came our senior year. Asking Kristen was not an option. In my foolish logic, I felt she was too valuable a friend to lose over the trappings and pressures of attending prom. I had set my sights on Iris. She was an adorable girl with an infectious laugh and a spunky nature. She seemed available then, and I knew her well enough to ask. After all, I had taught her how to drive a stick shift automobile along with my friend Ted. After school, we would jump in his Ford with the Hurst shifter and take a quick spin around Spaulding Ridge. Iris would ride in the middle, and either Ted or I would drive. We would accelerate, push in the clutch, and then holler shift, and Iris would slam it into gear. We had the radio blaring, the 8-track player loaded with the Beach Boys, and us singing along at the top of our lungs. The ride only lasted about 15 minutes, but we enjoyed it and looked forward to it, especially in the spring weather when we could roll down the windows. Iris eventually became the driver, which meant Ted and I would have to sit by each other, or one of us would ride in the back seat. Oh well, that ended all possibilities.

So, without all the trepidation surrounding my first attempt at asking a girl to the prom, I went up to Iris at her locker and asked her to the Dance. She looked shocked but said she couldn't go because she would be out of town. Not the answer I was hoping for, but I could live with it. On the bright side, no one could take my chair for this year's next " Risk " game. I never let anyone else know I had asked her, so there was nothing to discuss during our bull sessions. No harm, no foul.

Being the senior class president did have some responsibilities, and it also had some expectations, both stated and assumed. I was asked if I would attend and, if not, if I would be willing to take tickets at the door. There were few volunteers, and class officers were expected to offer their services for school activities as much as possible. How could I refuse? At least, it would be different than the reject party. Seeing all the couples arrive was unexpectedly fun. Many of my classmates were decked out in pastel blue, lime green, and even orange tuxedos.

Of course, the girls had dresses to match, and it was nice to see them in something other than a pair of jeans. I welcomed them to the event and exchanged silly small talk, wink, or an inside joke with those in my circle of friends. Then it happened. Like it had been set up on Candid Camera, Iris came in with her date. Her eyes met mine, and she flashed a quick sheepish grin. When I asked her, the girl would be out of town, but here she was, with someone else. I fought my desire to scream, "Are you kidding me?" Instead, with a phony smile, I gathered myself and welcomed them to the dance and told Iris how great it was that she could make it back to town in time to attend the dance.

As the last couple had arrived, my duties as a ticket taker, doorman, and greeter were through. I had planned on sitting in the bleachers to watch the night's events like prom guests were welcome to do, but the "Iris Event" shut down that idea. I left the school and drove around town for a little while, listening to the radio. I had to collect my thoughts about what had occurred earlier. Was I pissed? Sort of. Was I hurt? Maybe a little. Did I think less of Iris? In a way, yes. I still had no clue how girls think. I still felt like I needed to learn to keep my place and not put myself out there again. The ship that was my self-esteem had two holes blown in the side, and a third would sink it entirely.

As our senior year was winding down, all the things that had been firsts just a couple of years ago were becoming lasts. There was the last homecoming, winter carnival, basketball game, Christmas concert, and so on.

The year was coming to a close. The only thing left for us seniors was to prepare for the week of graduation. Everyone was getting their senior picture back and passing them around. We had gotten our caps and gowns and were planning our graduation parties. Nearly 80% of our class had plans to go to college after high school. Ryan would be playing football at Luther College in Iowa. I had visited the campus with him the summer before, and it looked like a great place. Not being a football player, I figured it wouldn't be my place. For the first time in years, he and I wouldn't be hanging out together. Ellen had planned to go to

Stout in Menomonie. It would be the first time she and Ryan wouldn't go to school together. Everyone wondered how this would affect "The Couple" in our class.

Kristen would be going to Concordia College in Moorhead, MN, like all her brothers and sisters before her. I had applied and been accepted to 3 different schools: UMD in Duluth, Minnesota, University of Wisconsin-Madison, and a small private college in La Crosse, WI, called Viterbo. I applied there because I won a small scholarship from them, and my close friend Ted and I had talked about going there together. Just a few weeks before the end of school, I decided to attend Viterbo. Ted and I could be roommates and ride back and forth from home together. Unfortunately, just after making that decision, Ted decided he would stay home and work construction.

It was too late for me to change my plans. I would have to go to Viterbo on my own. I would spend the summer scrambling to make new housing arrangements and searching for a new roommate. I thought many times about not going. I had much pressure at home to go to college. None of my older brothers and sisters had attended college. My parents were so proud of my high school achievements; there was no way they would understand if I didn't go.

Graduation night came, and since I was class president, I sat on the stage with the Valedictorian and local school officials, looking out at the class and the parents. My job was to call the class roll, signaling the students to come on the stage and get their diplomas from the superintendent. I constantly smiled as I looked at everyone's faces. I know many of them were hoping I would pull some stunt or tell one more joke for old-time's sake; I didn't dare. Looking at them during the ceremony, I thought about our years together and what we went through. Soon it came time to call the role. I stood at the podium and started calling the first of 157 names. Some of my friends shook my hand as they passed, while others just gave me a nod or a poke. Then I called Kristen Simpson. To my surprise and delight, Kristen stopped and kissed me. I'm sure I turned 100 shades of red. Somehow, that small gesture had made all the trials and tribulations of the last three years, worth it. What I believed in my heart was true. I had done the right things for the right reasons, and even if they hadn't turned out as I had expected, that was ok. I could go forward with newfound confidence, a profound affinity for my high school experience, and deep affection for my close friends who shared it with me.

Chapter Two:

Back of the Bus

The summer of '77 was the last hurrah for me and many friends. Like others before us, we had planned to take a trip across the country to see things we had never seen and spend time away from our parents. With no rules and nobody around who knew us, imagine the "wild things" we would do. Unfortunately, like most of the bull sessions of high school, this turned out to be much talk and not much action. Reality meant we needed to work and earn money for our college life ahead of us. We still had the occasional trip to Lake Arbutus to swim and water ski, but it was never with the whole group, and it just didn't feel the same. We were supposed to be grown up now, shedding the scales of youth and leaving our nicknames, jokes, classic stories, and the roles we played behind. We were becoming "serious" about our lives. I was struggling with my identity. I was always the comic relief for the group. It's hard to be funny by yourself. I had serious thoughts, but seriously dealing with the world never really worked for me.

The highlight of the summer for our family was a visit from my parent's closest friends from the time they were married—Kenny and Virginia from North Dakota and Bill and Nina Batty from Michigan. We learned over the years that Kenny walked my mother down the aisle and Bill was my dad's best man. Kenny and Bill had served with my father in the United States Air Force during the '50s and '60s. What made their visits enjoyable were the stories they would share of their early days together and how they told them. Kenny was hilarious.

I can only describe him as a Jonathan Winters type, complete with faces, voices, noises, and an infectious laugh. Bill was the "George Burns" of the group who always had a limerick, witty song, or just a quick retort to share that would make everyone laugh. Their wives were like my mother: caring, attentive, and sweet to everyone. What was also interesting is that our families were nearly the same size and make-up of boys and girls. Our ages were close as well. That meant we always had someone our age to play with when our families gathered. The older kids always gathered in someone's room and listened to records. The younger kids, like my twin sister Janet and I, often played outside or in the basement. Janet and I often played house with the Blazer's youngest girls, Beth and Carrie. Beth and I would typically be the wife and husband, and Carrie and Janet would be our kids. Sometimes, our pretend kids wouldn't listen to us and misbehave, requiring us to scold or ground them. This was based on our many observations of our older siblings' antics and the punishments our parents handed out.

All my older siblings had already left the nest; the same was true with Miller's and Batty's children. We were unsure what kids would be coming with their parents, but plans had already been made for the adults to occupy my and my sister's bedrooms. My dad also borrowed an old "School Bus Camper" from one of his friends and had set up his tent camper—the boys in the school bus and the girls in the tent camper. The trailers were parked out behind the house with extension cords providing just enough power to operate a couple of lights. There are no bathrooms or other facilities, just sleeping quarters.

The day arrived, and in drove Kenny and Virginia in their trademark blue Buick station wagon. They were scheduled to be following shortly. As our parents shared hugs and smiles, we kids stood awkwardly, waiting for instructions. It had been 5 or 6 years since we had seen each other. These past years were when children turned into young adults, and the changes could be dramatic. I had grown over 6 inches in height to 6'2" tall and no longer sported the traditional "military butch-style haircut," compliments of my father's barber skills. My sister, Janet, had become a young woman. For some reason, it didn't occur to me that Beth and Carrie would have also changed. Carrie was about the same except a little taller and heavier. Beth, however, was quite different. She went from a skinny tomboy who always wore t-shirts, shorts, flip flops, and kept her brown hair straight to a head-turning, fully-developed young woman, complete with make-up and form-fitting jeans. She still had a bright smile and happy eyes, but her hair was short and styled by someone other than her older sister. Our eyes met; there was a momentary element of surprise followed by a smile acknowledging the approval of our shared maturation.

At the direction of my mother, I took their suitcases and bags to the assigned rooms and then gave them a tour of our house, the bus, and the camper. Bill and Iris arrived shortly after that, and the same greeting only extended with the Blazers joining in. To my dismay, they did not bring their son Doug, who was the same age as me, but only their youngest daughter, affectionately known as "Pookie." As I recall, she was the youngest of all the families' kids and was about 9 or 10 that summer. She was an adorable, soft-spoken child with manners that the rest of us never learned. She also looked like a little "Indian Princess" with jet-black hair, darker skin, and pearl-white teeth. Her parents kept her close to them and doted on her every need. I was hoping Doug would have come with them because it would have given me a chance to do boy things like fish, play ball, bike, and talk nonsense with someone other than the girls. His absence left me wondering what I would do for the next few days.

The days were unscheduled; the routine saw adults rising first, taking turns in our sole bathroom, then gathering for morning coffee and breakfast prepared by the women.

Then, small talk took place, followed by suggestions for the day's activities. Dad once offered a tour of a few of the local sights that would be of interest, so we caravanned down to the dam, out to the "Pow Wow" grounds, and then spent the afternoon at "Lake Arbutus" for swimming and a picnic. Every evening, the adults grilled supper and drank while playing cards. Meanwhile, the kids gathered in the campers to pass the time. They played board games, listened to music, or talked among themselves as the adults socialized. The children entertained themselves with little supervision, only checking in occasionally to see if the adults needed help. After supper, the kids often returned to the campers to continue their activities late into the night. The evenings passed quickly, with both generations enjoying their separate social circles under the summer sky. There was plenty of pop and snacks for all. I missed Doug's presence a little less each evening as time spent with Beth was more enjoyable than expected. We were always part of the larger crowd, but we exchanged glances and laughs that grew in intensity with each passing day.

As the final night of the stay approached, the adults let it known that they were going out for dinner and then "painting the town" as they had in the old days. We, kids, could bake pizzas and do whatever we wished if we didn't leave the house. They even indicated that if we wanted a beer or two, we were allowed but limited to that number. This shocked me and my sister, as my folks usually didn't encourage us to drink. That was due to my older brothers' excessive behavior in their teens. I gladly complied as I didn't want to hear my father's lectures late into the night, followed by a purposeful early wake-up call for the "drunks." The next day, the usually hung-over participants were treated to some heavy physical work that would elicit a less than pleasant purging of the previous night's consumptions. So, we made our pizzas, played loud music, danced, and laughed about everything. Beth suggested we take up our parents' offer on the beer.

We each grabbed our two bottles and began drinking. Beth and Carrie seemed to have an acquired taste as they slammed their two bottles quickly. Janet and I sipped ours over the next hour. I didn't care that much for the taste of beer. However, even a couple would provide a pleasant attitude adjustment and easing of inhibitions. Then the phone rang, and it was my friend, Ryan. He wondered if I was interested in making a few dollars in the morning, helping his dad move some things to his warehouse. He said the day would start early, so be at his house by 7:00 a.m. I needed the money and had previously done many odd jobs for Ryan's dad. He paid well and often included a free lunch. The Blazers and Battys were leaving the next day anyway, so my obligation to be home was over. After that call, I saw the clock and realized it was nearly 11:00 pm. I finished my beers and then announced that I was turning in due to the early morning of work ahead. I let Beth, Carrie, and Pookie know how nice it was to have them visit and, if I didn't see them tomorrow, to have a safe trip home. Beth looked disappointed, but she and the girls played more music and danced. I headed to my bunk in the back of the bus, set my trusty Westclox wind-up alarm with the luminescent dial, and crawled under the covers, thinking about tomorrow.

Sometime later, I was awakened by a tapping on the bus's back door and a loud whisper of "Jay." Looking at the clock, it was just about 2:30 a.m., and I wondered who it was. Then, I thought it might be my mother letting me know they were home and checking how the evening went. I shuffled to the back door and opened it, expecting my mother to be standing there. To my surprise, at the bottom of the steps stood Beth. She was wearing a short, sheer white nightgown lightly touched by the moonlight, giving her a spectral glow. I asked her what was wrong. She said she couldn't sleep and wondered if she could come in and talk for a while. Still slightly asleep and unsure what to say, I said come on in.

As she climbed the stairs and came closer, the fact that she was wearing nothing under her nightgown became more evident and slapped any sleep out of my eyes. I quickly crawled under the blanket of my bunk as I realized I was wearing only my boxer shorts and t-shirt, and outside of my sister or mother, no female had ever seen me in my nighttime attire. She sat on the bunk across the aisle from mine and talked about how much fun she had early in the evening. I was glad that there was so little light on the bus, making it easier for me to hide my preoccupation with what her nightgown revealed. I was so ecstatically surprised that I had no idea what to say when it was my turn. No problem; she wasn't all that interested in my intellectual musings anyway. She said she was cold and asked if it would be possible to crawl under my blanket to warm up. Was this some joke? My mind was racing and trying to come up with the correct answer. I said yes, and she gleefully hopped in, pressing herself against me as close as possible. We were now face to face, only inches apart. All the talking ended in that moment. We began to kiss each other. Softly at first, as if to say, is this ok with you? Soon, the intensity increased, and she grabbed my hand and placed it on her breast. I caressed her and let instinct guide me to investigate the rest of her body. I paused slightly, expecting her to set the boundaries for my anatomy lesson by saying – something like – "no" or "stop." Instead, she began her voyage of discovering what I had to offer.

As she reached down, she found what she was looking for. In the excitement, I had become aroused to break the seams of my boxer shorts. It never occurred to me that the freedom and convenience boxer shorts offered also came with the lack of restraint jockey shorts managed in such cases. So, me protruding from my shorts gave her the cue she sought. She pushed me onto my back and quickly removed her nightgown and panties. Then, deftly and gently, she took a position on top of me. Slowly, she performed her pelvic exercise, occasionally gasping to catch her breath. I lay motionless, fixated on her face and eyes. She smiled the same smile and had the same look in her eyes that we shared on the day of her arrival. Then, she picked up the pace as if under some time constraint. This was now a full-out sprint to the finish, and I could no longer lay motionless. After a few minutes, I knew what was about to happen. I had no control over the release of my male genetic material. I expected that to stop her. What happened next was just the opposite. She shifted into yet another gear, and for the next two or three minutes, she writhed feverishly, groaned, and moaned, making noises I was sure would wake up the girls in the camper or cause the neighbor's dog to start barking. Then, suddenly, she stiffened straight up, shuddered as if she had been hit by a cold wind, and took a deep breath, holding it for what seemed like an hour. She released her breath and fell forward in a heap on top of me. She was limp and wringing, wet with sweat. Once again, I lay motionless, trying to grasp what had just happened and recover from my physical exertion. Still, neither of us spoke a word. I felt like I might fall asleep, and she might do the same.

I spoke her name, "Beth." She lifted her head just high enough to look me in the face and leaned forward, kissing me. She then arose from the bunk, found her nightgown, dressed, and headed for the back door, "See you tomorrow," she said as she exited, clicking the handle shut behind her. I stared into the darkness, dazed, confused, strangely satisfied, wondering what tomorrow would bring. I looked at the alarm's glowing hands, and it was 3:30 AM.

What seemed like a second later, I was awakened by the annoying clanging of the alarm clock. How could it be 6:30 AM already? I was exhausted and feeling a little nauseous. A strange and unfamiliar odor was hanging like the morning fog. As I got up from the bunk, I saw the source of the smell displayed in all its glory on the bedsheet. I looked down at my shorts and t-shirt, and an even greater smearing of the night's unholy activities stained the pure white of the fabric. I began to panic. I had to find a way to clean the sheets and change my underwear before I went to Ryan's house. I was afraid of someone smelling what I could. I removed my t-shirt and, using the back with some water from a plastic bottle, scrubbed the sheet until there was no noticeable stain. Then, I slipped on my cut-offs and sneaked into the house's back porch to the laundry room. Fortunately, a stack of my clothes on the dryer included a fresh change of underwear. I changed right there, and instead of putting my clothes into the hamper, I dug into the bottom of the garbage can under the scrub sink and hid my dirty sin-filled boxers and a t-shirt under the old detergent bottles and wads of dryer lint. I had to eliminate the chance that my mother would see them in the hamper and realize what her son had been up to. I finished dressing and headed to Ryan's as quickly as I could. It was already 7:00 a.m.

I arrived at Ryan's and went inside as I had done for years. I was one of the family since 12, so I rarely knocked on the front door. Standing in the kitchen was Ryan and his dad. He gave me some good-natured grief for not being exactly on time and wondered what I was doing all night. I told him I was drinking and chasing women like always. He laughed and said that's what he thought; if only he had known how close to the truth my excuse was.

We jumped into his green Ford Country Squire station wagon and headed North toward the warehouse. I was riding in the backseat and closed my eyes, trying to catch up on sleep. There was no rest to be had as my mind repeatedly replayed the night. My mind raced as my actions' potential consequences started hitting me. What if Beth told her sister and the news made it to her parents? How would it fly that their best friend's son had his way with their daughter? What if she turned out to be pregnant? Suddenly, I felt sick to my stomach and asked Ryan's dad to pull over because I was going to puke. He did, and I rolled out of the backseat, got down on all fours, and heaved into the ditch. After retching for a few minutes, I felt better and collapsed into the car. The rest of the day, I was not much help. I would work for a while and then have another episode. Finally, at about 3:00 PM, we were finished and stopped for a soda at a local watering hole.

The fluids seemed to help, and I started to feel normal again. Ryan's dad excused himself for a moment, and it was at that opportunity that I shared with Ryan the previous evening's events. I wasn't bragging like I was part of the bull sessions, but curious for a reaction. Ryan was surprised and chuckled slightly at the details I presented. He asked if I was going to see her again. I didn't know. Ryan's dad returned, and we loaded into the vehicle and drove home. I quickly got in my car at Ryan's and headed to my house. Upon arriving, I noticed the Blazer's and Batty's vehicles were gone. I went into the house and asked my mom if they had left for good. She said yes and wondered if we had a good time the night before. She had no idea about what had transpired. I told her about the night and the beer but left out what had happened after I went to bed. Then, she asked if I would help clean up around the house so we could get back to our regular arrangement. I did and had to take a moment to reflect when that big blue school bus camper left the yard.

Thank goodness my fears about what could have happened never materialized. I spent many quiet times reliving that night and wondering why Beth knocked on the bus door. I also asked if Beth had any feelings for me. It would have been nice to think our actions were somehow based on an underlying emotional connection. I had always thought that making love was supposed to be an expression between two people deeply committed to each other. In my mind, I guessed it would have made it more right than wrong. I never heard from or saw Beth again. I never spoke about that night again to anyone. What we shared changed me and affected my relationships for the rest of my life.

August arrived, and my sister and I were to celebrate our 18th birthday on the 8th. My mother offered to let us throw an "adult birthday party" if we wished. We had been sharing our birthdays all our lives and decided that maybe we could finally skip the "twins" birthday parties. I loved my sister, and she loved me, but as close as we were as small children, we had separated as teens and struggled to do much together anymore. We had some of the same friends but never really "hung out" with each other's group. We had other issues that brothers and sisters had, but we also had the unique situation of being in the same class and sharing a car to drive, which often led to more conflict. The only thing we did agree upon was not to snitch on each other. Our parents knew we could communicate often without speaking and, for our sake, never pitted one of us against the other. I think they admired our twin commitment to each other. As the distance increased, we were still connected in a special way. My mother often commented over the years how if one of us would call home, it wouldn't be long, sometimes within the hour, that the other would call. I have to say that outside of my mother, my twin sister, Janet, is the only person who has an innate knowledge of how I "tick" and who I am. In one way, it is comforting and beautiful to think about and sometimes scary to have somebody who can get inside your head.

I arrived home one evening after work, and my mother pointed out that I had a letter. I hardly ever got mail and wondered who could be writing to me. The return address read David Stoeffler from Mt. Hope, WI. I opened the envelope to find a 3-page letter neatly handwritten on yellow legal notepad papers. David introduced himself in the greeting and then reminded me that we had met before. Earlier in the school year, Black River Falls High School faced Mt. Hope High on the televised quiz show "High Quiz Bowl." A local takeoff on the nationally televised "College Bowl."

Four team members were asked various questions on educational subjects and were required to "ring in" with the chance to provide the correct answer. Points were awarded for correct answers or deducted for incorrect answers. There were bonus questions, and after the allotted ½ hour, the team with the most points would be the winner. David reminded me that I had answered the first question of our competition and how he thought their team might be in for a long night. They drubbed us with a score of something like 395 to 65. Anyway, he explained that he had gotten my name from Viterbo College admissions as one of the incoming first-year students and wondered if I would like to be roommates. I was thrilled that I might not have to search for a roommate when I arrived, and it would be great to have some conversations before school. He gave me his phone number and invited me to call to respond to his request. I called, and we had a delightful conversation; it felt like I was talking to someone I had known for a long time. We agreed to be "roomies" and would meet later that month at move-in.

The day came to a head off to Viterbo. As strange as it sounds, I had never visited Viterbo College before going there. The only two reasons for even applying to Viterbo were the High Quiz Bowl Scholarship, which was a whopping two-hundred dollars, and my close friend Ted agreed to go, and we could be roommates. Ted had backed out, and I had no idea what to major in. I was going to avoid disappointing my parents. We rolled up to the front of Treacy House, a small two-story apartment building, very non-descript versus the surrounding neighborhood. I knew I was in apartment three, so I searched for it while my mother and father waited in the car. It was in the middle of the first-floor hallway, so I went in. I was pleasantly surprised to see a living room, dining area, kitchen area, three bedrooms, and a full bath.

Down the hallway from the far bedroom came a tall, thin young man with blonde hair, a bright smile, and a cherub-like appearance. He was very angular with a sharp nose, pronounced Adam's apple, and cheeks with a permanent rose blush. It was David. He reached out his hand, and we greeted each other. I told him my parents were outside and I needed to get them and my stuff. I went back out, gathered my belongings from the trunk of the car, and carried everything into the apartment with my parent's help.

I introduced David to my folks, and they exchanged small talk while I carried my stuff down to the room David and I would share. As I returned, I could hear some laughter as my dad explained to David that I wasn't weaned until I was six years old. He had told this joke my whole life and was compelled to share it anytime I was with my friends. I indicated that everything was in and it was probably time for them to go as other kids would need to park out front and move in. Dad said goodbye to David and said it was nice to meet him. He left without saying anything to me. My mother looked at me and fought back her emotions. She asked if there was anything else I needed. I assured her I would be fine, then hugged and kissed her goodbye. David helped me carry a few remaining items to our room and showed me the arrangement, asking if I preferred the top or bottom bunk. I told him I was okay with the top unless he objected. We talked and agreed to buy matching bedspreads later to enhance the room's appearance.

Soon, more roommates were arriving. Jeff was the next—a shorter, dark, wavy-haired kid from Dubuque, Iowa. Jeff made a point of telling me he was a theater major. I had no clue what that meant. He unpacked all kinds of records of Show Tunes and had no inhibition about singing selections from Broadway the whole time he set up his room. Then, two additional guys named David arrived. One was a tall, red-headed

Irishman, Dave Donovan, from New Albin, Iowa, and the other was a tall, stocky German from Adams Friendship, Dave Weingarten. They had already communicated and decided to share a room as one would major in Biology and the other in Nursing. The final arrival was a hometown La Crosse kid named Leo Schneider. Leo and his identical twin brother Larry were attending Viterbo in religious studies with the potential of becoming priests. They both were accomplished orchestral musicians and ultra-nice people. Leo would room with Jeff, and Larry was in another apartment. They appeared to me as Jewish accountants with dark hair and round John Lennon wire-rimmed glasses. Everyone talked to each other over the next few hours about majors, family, and high schools, and it seemed we would all get along quite well.

That afternoon, I visited Murphy Center and met with my advisor to finalize registration and my class schedule. I was attending as an "undeclared" student, meaning I had not picked a major field of study. I thought about nursing, education, pre-law, etc. I needed to know more before I could pull the trigger on any of them. I figured I had time as first-year students typically have required graduation subjects anyway. I wish someone in my family had attended college before I did. There was no way I could imagine how this would turn out!

My roommate David and I spent the rest of that evening eating pizza at Happy Joe's and purchasing our matching bedspreads at Penney's. I learned that David was going to be a Journalism Major. He told me he had already contacted the editor of the La Crosse Tribune for advice and also sought out the advisors of the Viterbo College newspaper, the "Lumen." David ended up becoming the paper's editor and writing a weekly editorial. David also confided in me that he had a high school sweetheart who lived in Patch Grove, Wisconsin. Her name was Rose, and it was more than apparent that he was head over heels in love with her. As we settled in that first night, we talked for hours about our lives and dreams after lights out. I was impressed with David's preparedness and plans for his future. On day one, he organized his plans and remained motivated to achieve his goals without losing focus. In contrast, I had no plan and was flying by the seat of my pants, making decisions with no thought of tomorrow. My most significant decision so far was taking the top bunk. Practical, but hardly life-altering. It would be a trend that continued.

The next day was a Friday and a chance for freshmen students to finalize their move-in and schedules before classes started on Monday. We just hung out around the apartment, decided about cable TV, and got our phones hooked up. We discussed what the furniture arrangement would be and shared life stories. Around 11:00 AM, our phone rang, and it was for me. I had no idea who could be on the line. I answered, and the voice on the other end said, "Hello, Jay, this is Father Recker from the Theater Arts department here at Viterbo. Can I talk to you briefly about your undeclared major status?"

I said, "Sure, that's fine. What about it?" Well, for the next 20 minutes, he advised that I should consider picking a major even if I wasn't sure because most of the majors required freshman credits of some kind. Certain classes wouldn't be offered every semester. This meant that it might take longer than four years to complete a major due to schedule conflicts. I told him no one had advised me of that before registration. He then said he pulled my records and noticed that I had been very active in high school drama and musicals and even had been named in "Who's Who Among High School Music Students." Would I be interested in trying out Theater Arts as a major? He felt I would do well and enjoy the classes and participation in Viterbo's productions. He also offered to adjust my class schedule so I could have the basics most first-year students needed and credit classes that Theater Majors needed their first year. He said if I didn't care for theater after the first semester, I could always pick a different major. He was very persuasive and entirely complimentary about what he saw in my file. So, I asked what did I have to do? He said yes, and he would take care of everything else. After a few moments of thinking, I agreed. He said, "Wonderful," and to just stop by his office in the Fine Arts Center Monday morning, and he would give me my new schedule and show me the "Green Room," which was the gathering spot for all the theater majors. We said goodbye, and just that quickly, I was no longer on my own.

I mentioned it to Jeff, and he was thrilled that he and I would be able to share classes and talk "Theater." I liked Jeff. He was kind, funny, polite, and sensitive. On the other hand, he was so energetic and obsessed with the theater that he could be annoying in extended interactions. He continuously sang Show Tune as he danced around the apartment. I was hoping he was the exception and not the rule of the other theater majors I would be meeting. That weekend, I walked around campus, meeting other kids, attending the freshman mixer at the college pub, and getting to know my roommates.

Monday morning came, and I entered the first floor of the Fine Arts Center. About halfway down the hallway, on the left, were the Theater Arts Chairperson's and Assistant Chairperson's offices. I approached the chairperson's doorway, stuck my head in, and said, "Father Recker, I'm Jay Eddy. You told me to stop in here this morning."

Arising from behind a large oak desk and out of a black leather wingback chair, Father Recker smiled, extended his hand, and said, "Yes, Good Morning. Come in." We shook hands, and he invited me to sit down. I was surprised that he was not dressed in his traditional priestly vestments. Instead, he wore a dark gray knit polo and blue corduroy slacks. He wore shiny brown penny loafers, complete with the bright copper penny. He was a slim man of above average height, with a large, slightly round nose, pockmarked skin, George Jetson-styled dark hair with gray touched temples, and huge Charles Nelson Reilly eyeglasses. His mouth was somewhat crooked, and his voice was strong with a pronounced nasal twang. He welcomed me to the department and commented on not realizing how big I was. "That's great!" He said, "We need someone with some size for the stage and to work in our scene shop."

He gave me my schedule and explained some more about the department. Then, he took me next door to the assistant chairperson's office.

"Sister," he said, "This big boy" (A term he would use to refer to me for the rest of my career at Viterbo) is our newest student in the theater department."

"Jay Eddy, this is Sister Marie Leon," he said with a formal introductory tone.

Sister Marie Leon was a tiny little woman with a natural, sweet smile that reminded me of nearly anyone's grandmother or aunt. She wore a white flower-printed dress, glasses, black shoes, and a silver medallion of some religious symbol. I later learned that all the "Sisters of Perpetual Adoration" wore that medallion, who occupied St. Rose Convent, were connected to the college. She greeted me, said she was happy that I would be part of the department, and wished me great success. I was taken aback by the fact that she dressed in regular street clothes, not traditional ones.

Father added, "Let's go across the hall to the "Green Room," and I will show you where our theater students gather to study."

The "Green Room" wasn't green at all. It was a converted classroom with one block wall, a wall with windows, a wall with a chalkboard that curtains had covered, and one wall of bookshelves decorated with assorted theater books and nick-nacks. The walls had numerous mounted black and white photos of Viterbo Theater Productions of the recent past and others looking like they might have been 50-plus years old. There were no desks in the room but an assortment of garage sale couches and chairs, none of which matched, and many showed signs of upholstery repair done by unskilled labor. As mismatched as the furniture appeared, the kids occupying the room were even more diverse. They could have come from the island of misfit toys. Father introduced me and then returned to his office. I found a chair near one of the corners and sat down to take in the atmosphere.

Three kids were sitting on a couch across the room, smoking and sharing an ashtray on the table before them. Nearly every kid in the room looked like they shopped at the Salvation Army—lots of jeans, flannel shirts, unkempt hairstyles, and sleep-deprived faces offering friendly smiles. No other newcomer student was in the room, so all these kids were upperclassmen. We talked for a while, and they quizzed me about my high school career while sharing their life stories as Viterbo Theater Majors. Along with the advice were caution about others not there, Father Recker and Sister Marie Leon. Soon it was time to say goodbye; nice to meet you; see you later, and head off to class. All I could think was how different this group seemed from my high school bunch. Interesting.

Chapter Three:

Have Another Beer

The first class for Theater Major beginners was called "Introduction to Theater Arts" and was taught by Father Recker. It is only available to first-year theater students. Entering the room, I expected to find 20 to 30 kids. To my surprise, there were only four. Two girls and two boys.

One of the boys was my roommate, Jeff. The other was Roger Ward, a very strange-looking fellow from the Milwaukee area. If you have ever watched the Muppet show, you might think you have seen a character that looked like Roger. He was about 5 feet tall, bent slightly forward, and had a sizeable balding spot on the top of his head with skinny, straight strings of hair sprouting around it. They almost appeared to be drawn on, as you would see in a drawing done by a small child. He had huge red lips and oversized glasses of an evident powerful magnification. A small amount of drool gathered on the corners of his mouth when he spoke. As I learned later in conversations, he was also very animated. He often smoked a cigarette and waved it around like a maestro's baton to emphasize one word or another. He also had an accented big-city tone, making you think he might be from Brooklyn or the Bronx. He was a friendly kid, but I couldn't relate to him and his sense of humor.

The first girl I noticed was a doll-faced redhead with large blue eyes. Her name was Mary Hare. She was from Lodi, Wisconsin, home of the famous Tom Wopat of the "Dukes of Hazzard." I found it ironic that Mary's last name was "Hare" because she often had a look on her face of a rabbit in the backyard who realized they had been spotted and stayed completely still, but their eyes spoke of panic. At the time, I wondered if she would have the courage to step onto a stage. The other girl just so happened to be a redhead as well. Her name was Becky Wise from Chatfield, Minnesota. She was small in height and stature with a Dorothy Hamill haircut, freckled face and arms, and, like myself, had bright green eyes and a serious look on her face. She was noticeably well dressed compared to the rest of us and seemed comfortable with where she was, as if she had been here before. Out of the 40-plus theater majors, we were the new crop of freshmen, five in total.

The first couple of weeks of school were hectic, trying to get into the habit of college life, free time, study time, and learning my work-study job. I was assigned as a chalkboard and eraser cleaner in the Murphy Center. On Tuesday and Thursday evenings, after the last class, I would go into the rooms, erase the chalkboards, clean them with a special spray and rag made for such a task, and then take the foot-long rubber erasers down to the end of the hall to a janitor closet and run them through this eraser cleaning machine. It looked like a jointer table with a vast vacuum mounted underneath. It did a great job but made an ear splitting sound. Then, I returned the erasers and headed home. For this, I was paid $2.30 an hour.

Most of my non-theater classes were full, with about 30 kids each. I had never really had to study in high school, but so far, college was kicking my backside. I struggled with how much reading I had to do and having the discipline to set aside time to do the work. I also was not an excellent note-taker and found that as good as my memory had been in my high school days, I was overwhelmed with the sheer amount of information. Luckily, David was my roommate. He had mastered all those study skills and was quite comfortable with the process. He took fabulous notes and was willing to help me as needed. I was so impressed with his skills and ambition. No wonder his team beat us by 300+ points in the High Quiz Bowl.

The other great thing about David is that he had a sharp wit and enjoyed throwing out some light-hearted banter that always made the study session more enjoyable. We spent many hours laughing and seeing who could top the other with some observation. As it turned out, David became the editor of the "Lumen," the college paper. Weekly, he would write an editorial and cover a specific topic of college life or offer an opinion on the world's happenings.

One week, he was looking for something to help change his regular editorial, and I came up with an idea. I said why don't you offer some story about your roommate. Make him (me) have some funny habits or viewpoints. So, we brainstormed and started with a roommate who bragged about beating his dog in chess in 3 out of 5 games. It caught on, and people began asking David about his roommate and what other goofy things he did. A couple of times a month, David and I would devise some strange quirk or habit that readers loved to read and laugh about. Nearly every night, we would lay in the dark and talk about more serious things. David told me all about his girlfriend, Rose, and how much he loved and missed her. He went home most weekends so that he could see her. I told him about my less-than-exciting dating life but that I did have intense feelings for Kristen and never dared to tell her. In his thoughtful way, he finally convinced me to write her a letter and express how I felt. I sent it out and eagerly awaited a response, hoping we could rekindle a stronger relationship than our high school situation.

In the meantime, the theater department was gearing up for its first production of the year, and auditions would be taking place. I learned a few more of the kids in the department, and those who stayed around for the weekends often visited a local bar next to campus called "Wunderbar." The kids would gather and have a couple of 25-cent tappers or share a pitcher of beer and talk about their dreams of becoming a star. Don't let the name "Wunderbar" lead you to think of an establishment with champagne and a bubble machine fit for Lawrence Welk. This was the textbook definition of a dive. The front door was rarely closed, and neighborhood dogs occasionally wandered in for a treat or friendly attention. It was always dark regardless of the time of day and held onto a steady cloud of cigarette smoke. The only light of any consequence came from the assorted neon bar signs hung along the walls. It was probably better because real light might have shown how clean the bar glasses were.

The first theater department production of the year was "Harvey." Father Recker would be directing, and auditions were scheduled in the "Black Box" theater downstairs in the Fine Arts Center. I had never auditioned for a part in high school. I didn't know what to expect, and judging by the anxiety many of the kids seemed to be exhibiting, it would be a big deal.

It took place over a couple of nights and consisted of Father Recker calling on students to step to the stage and read certain character parts with each other. He would then call on another group and have them read the same or another scene. I read for one part that wasn't the lead. The cab driver came in at the end of the play in the second to last scene of the last act: one speech and two or three other lines. The next day the "callback" list was posted on the bulletin board in the hallway outside the green room. If your name was on it, you returned for another reading. If not, you didn't get a part and would be working on a technical aspect of the production. To my surprise, my name and Becky Wise's names were on the callback list; no other freshmen.

After callback night, the final cast list for the play with twelve parts was posted. I scanned the list eagerly, hoping to see my name. To my delight, I had been selected to play the cab driver. My friend Becky Wise had landed an even better role as Myrtle Mae Simmons, one of the main characters. Although my part was small, I was thrilled to be a part of the production. Becky and I congratulated each other, excited to start rehearsals together.

Pretty impressive for her, I thought. Some kids were very friendly and congratulated the cast, while others grumbled as they were obviously hurt or discouraged. I had no particular feeling either way. I should have been excited, but I just figured it was another play I would be in.

The girl who got the lead female part of Veta Louise was a senior named Jennifer Taylor. Jennifer was the best-looking female in the department and possibly in La Crosse. She was "Hollywood" beautiful. She had to have been a cheerleader, prom queen, or county fair princess at one time. Not a blemish on her pretty face. Her smile revealed perfectly straight, denture quality, sparkling white teeth, and she had the classic flowing "Candace Bergen" blonde hair. The rest of her features were as one would expect. She lived off campus with her boyfriend (later husband), Gary. I never got to know her that well. She went on after college to do television commercials. She had a reoccurring role on the popular soap opera "Edge of Night." It gave the rest of us hope that dreams can come true. Most would later learn that talent is only part of the equation, and the other is God-given good looks. They can't teach that at college. It's like that basketball coach who had a player needing more skills. The kid was 7 feet tall, and the coach said, "You can't teach 7 feet."

Rehearsals would begin the following week on the main stage and run for about six weeks until opening night in October. With such a small part, I wasn't needed most days and only showed up for the initial read-through and a couple of nights of "blocking."

Blocking is just the plan for the characters' movements and setting the lines that would be the cue for those movements—my nights stayed relatively the same as before, doing classwork after supper and then watching TV or playing ping pong with Jeff in the basement of Treacy House. On the weekends, we would do cleaning, laundry, and maybe go to Pettibone Park or Grandad's Bluff to soak up the scenery and have a few beers.

One day, I arrived home after classes and checked the kitchen table for mail. I usually never had any, but even junk mail feels good sometimes. Sure enough, there was a letter for me from Kristen with her return address at Concordia College. I quickly took it into my room and closed the door to read it. It was filled with all kinds of descriptions of her experiences at school, along with references to some of our high school days. She asked me about how things were going at Viterbo. There was nothing, however, addressing my feelings for her and no answers to questions I had asked about her feelings for me. It was as if she hadn't even seen them in my letter. My heart sank, and I felt almost ashamed of even writing her in the first place. I had hoped that distance would allow us to say things to each other that we might not be comfortable saying face to face. We also didn't have the peer group hovering over us, offering their reactions or opinions.

A wave of anguish washed over me, leaving me shaken to my core. I was utterly devastated and needed time to pull myself together. The grief was so raw that the rest of the day dragged by as I struggled to regain composure after the distressing news. My wounded heart ached as I fought to carry on through the sadness.

I decided a mid-week visit to Wunderbar would provide the salve needed to heal this wound. It emphasized that I was alone and that my desire to have someone, namely a girlfriend, to share my deeper personal feelings may not happen for me. I liked college less and less with each day. Funny "Jay" needed more and more Wunderbar visits to keep him on top of his wit and energize his persona. It was not the ideal prescription, to say the least. I was getting by in school. Classwork was challenging, but I was hanging in there and getting used to how much work it would be to pull the grades I was used to in high school. The competition was a lot tougher also. I realized some of these kids were here to get ahead in life, and they had the desire and discipline to do what it would take to make it happen.

Then came the last two weeks of rehearsal for our production, and it was my turn to get on stage. Father Recker bellowed from somewhere in the theater the first night I came out on cue and started delivering my lines, "Stop! What kind of crap was that cabbie?"

"All I am hearing are lines."

"Haven't you done anything to develop your character?"

His tone was very harsh and condescending. I felt like a total idiot. He gave me some directions and said, "Come back here tomorrow with something."

We finished the scene, and I made my exit. I found a chair backstage and sat there, totally dumbfounded. I had done many plays before coming to Viterbo, both in high school and community theater and had never been jumped on like that. I put my head down and my face in my hands, thinking about what a mess I had made of my life. One of the other cast members was backstage and noticed me sitting there. Her name was Lynne Vosen from La Farge, Wisconsin. She was a super friendly gal who always had a smile and a nurturing, almost big sister-like attitude with everyone. She came over to me and asked if I was all right. I told her that I think I am going to drop out. I didn't know I could go back out on that stage again. She told me she had been through the same thing her first year. She also said that the other kids in the department had commented on how much they liked me and thought I would be terrific. I don't know if that was true, but it was nice to hear. She offered to help me in the green room the next day to find something that would work. I thanked her, but I wasn't sure if I would stay and would need to consider it.

After rehearsal, many theater kids ventured into the Wunderbar to talk about the evening's events and how they thought the play was coming. I joined them to listen and drank enough so that I could sleep that night. The thought of having to tell my mother and father that I wanted to come home and leave school kept circling in my mind. My mother would undoubtedly be supportive, understanding, and maybe slightly disappointed. My dad would be pissed and find some way to question what the hell was wrong with me for picking theater in the first place. He hated the idea of college and had used the term "educated idiot" a thousand times. He then would go into his speech about being poor as a kid and working on the farm, and having his dad be hard on him so they could make it in the world. That was followed by his story of working for a dollar a day out West as a teenager on the wheat farms, then coming home and deciding at 17 that he was going into the service.

In his mind, the military was the "best damn thing" he ever did, and every kid should have to serve. He didn't realize that we grew up on the bases he served at, and for most of our lives, we felt like we had performed as well. Not a day would go by that Sgt. Eddy didn't give his kids some order intended for adult males, complete with phrases like, "Get your dumb ass in gear."

Wow, how much beer is this going to take?

Chapter Four:

Expanding the Circle

Lucky for me, David was still awake when I arrived back to my room. I gave him the play-by-play of the evening and how I was feeling. He talked me into sticking it out in school with his usual wisdom and caring tone. He jokingly said he needed me for his roommate, or his editorials would fall flat. He also reminded me that I could change majors after the semester if things didn't improve, and I wouldn't waste the money or the time I had already invested. On a lighter note, he said he was hoping that I was going to go to the Marion Hall "Halloween Party" later in the month with him. He had an idea that we could go as brothers. "Howdy Doody," and his brother, "Do Your Doody." He said that even though he wasn't looking for another girl, there would undoubtedly be plenty of them there that night, and I should keep my eyes open. I felt better and not so alone. David had become a real friend whom I could trust. I would have to hang in there and see how things worked out. I was also pumped about the Halloween Party and the fun he and I could have as one of the "Doody Brothers."

The next day in the green room, another kindness came my way. Becky Wise, the only other freshman in the production and doing very well in her role, came over to speak with me. She had heard from Lynne of my despair and wanted to let me know that she thought I should reconsider. I told her I was impressed with her efforts and wondered how she knew so much about what to do. She told me that her family was theater-oriented. Her older brother had graduated from Northwestern in Chicago with a degree in theater, and he had starred and directed the local "Western Days" musicals in Chatfield for many years. Her mother and father had also taken prominent roles, and her brother had given her and them all kinds of instruction on character development and theater. That's where her interest came from and enabled her to hit the ground running more or less when she arrived at Viterbo. Her parents were very supportive, and she had no worries about the outcome.

As she spoke, I was taken by her voice and the quiet surety in her delivery. I found the actual tone of her voice quite attractive. It was much like June Allyson with a mix of child-like sweetness and Bernadette Peter's sensualness. She could easily express humor, sorrow, surprise, or satire with a slight tone change. We talked more about my character, and she agreed to help me at rehearsals when not on stage. I told her it would be nice to have someone to talk with about anything during rehearsals. It was also great because we shared the same theater classes. As she left, I thanked her for offering and said I would see her later. After our visit, I looked at her more during classes and thought about her away from rehearsals and school.

Like every amateur actor, I had the idea that the number of lines my character had equated to how important my character was in the play. In the case of the "Cab Driver" in Harvey, I learned the exact opposite. The cab driver's speech toward the end of the play might be the most important in the story. Here, the playwright makes her most extraordinary statement on the human condition and gathers awareness in the audience and the story's main characters of what reality means. I thanked Becky and Lynne both for helping me make this discovery. It also helped me understand why Father Recker was so intent on me delivering this message through this character. He placed great confidence in my abilities and hoped I wouldn't disappoint him. After understanding this, I felt I needed to commit to being a "Theater Major." From then on, I worked hard to learn what being an actor meant. Before that, I had always relied on my ability to mimic or impersonate. There is a giant leap from there to character development. It requires understanding the who, what, and why of a character.

Finding the motivations behind a character's actions is the basis for good character development. It is also an excellent foundation for understanding the human condition. As I continued to dive into my study, I found understanding why people do what they do to be the most fascinating part of the theater. I made it through the role of the Cab Driver and was looking forward to how I might be challenged in the future.

David and I were preparing for our Halloween party premiere of the "Doody Brothers" when my roommate, Jeff, asked if we were taking dates. David told him we weren't but thought we would mingle with whoever was there and maybe dance with a few girls. Then, Jeff said to me something I thought was strange. He asked me why I didn't ask Becky Wise from the theater department to the dance. He thought she was cute and noticed that she and I had been talking a lot over the past few weeks.

I think Jeff had a little crush on her, but he thought maybe she and I were an item. I told Jeff I agreed she was cute, but I didn't know she would be that interested in a Halloween party. However, I would talk to her if she was at the party. As it turned out, Becky was at the party and came over to our table. I suspected she wasn't in costume, but she did enjoy David and my effort with ours. We spent the evening talking, laughing, dancing, having a few drinks, and deciding by the time the night was over that we should see each other again. It was terrific, and in that one night, I had overcome the despair I felt just a few weeks ago. I had a future ahead of me, and I was finally able to let go of my high school experience. This college thing was going to work out.

The next few months flew by. I had a pretty well-established routine. Classwork was becoming more manageable. Becky and I spent more and more of our free time together. Our regular date time was usually Friday nights after she returned from work. She had gotten a job as "Breezy - the Clown" at the State Bank of La Crosse. Every Friday night, she would go down and dress up as Breezy and hand out balloons to kids, do face painting, or play games. It was a nice paying gig, and she enjoyed interacting with the kids who came. The bank was happy to have her as well. She did a great job. We had an understanding that I should stay away when she was working, and I was happy to accommodate her. It gave me a chance to take in "Happy Hour" at Wunderbar, then off to the cafeteria for "Friday Fish" just before they closed at 6:00 PM. Then, I went to my room to watch some TV or nap before Becky got off work around 8:00.

Many nights we would listen to music and talk about Friday afternoons and what happened at Theater Workshop. This class was mandatory for all theater majors and was the only theater class that occurred in all four years of school for theater majors. In the workshop, students would be asked to perform scenes as a group or an individual monologue assigned by Father Recker the week before. Once the performances took place, the rest of the students who didn't perform that week would critique along with Father Recker. This was tough because some students could be very critical, and performers often took comments personally. Father would take the position of commenting on the performance and students critiquing. It wasn't uncommon to have the class reactions that day spill over to Wunderbar at Happy Hour, or as it was often referred to, "Not So Happy Hour."

Becky and I often had conversations about the workshop events that day and the positive and negative reactions. We shared the same opinions quite often concerning specific performances. She was typically gentler in her remarks and always tried to find a positive review for everyone. I could be a little more sarcastic.

Our date nights often ended with me walking her back to Marion Hall, the girl's dorm, where we hid in the stairwell to the cafeteria. This was our lover's lane. It was dimly lit and offered privacy away from the building's main hallways and traffic areas. We would sit on the top step, kiss, and share our feelings for each other. Occasionally, our sessions would become heated to the point where we might loosen some clothing and do some "heavy petting," as it were. I wanted my touch to express my affection for her instead of what I had experienced with Beth. It was nice because Becky and I could talk about anything, including our physical relationship. We agreed that certain sexual things were off the table until we made a more significant commitment to each other in the future. It was comforting in one sense but not always easy as we were becoming closer and closer each day.

We were also doing pretty well in the theater department. I had gotten another small non-speaking part in the next production, "Becket," as Baron #4. It was one of those parts that anyone could have landed, and I think every male in the department was needed for the production. Becky was hitting it out of the park in the workshop. It was apparent to everyone that she was very talented and desired to get even better. I was also becoming known for my sense of humor and often did some of my best performances in the green room between classes. Father occasionally stopped in to take in my impersonations or character improvisations to see if I could crack up the group. I could tell he enjoyed my creativity and quick wit.

On the other hand, Becky and I learned that Father didn't want theater students dating each other. Many students would caution that if he found out about relationships within the department, those involved would not get parts together in shows. Becky and I were careful not to display our affections in his or Sister's presence. I didn't care what Father thought about my personal life, but I didn't want to ruin anything for Becky. Soon, the first semester was ending, and it was time to go home for Christmas break. I was looking forward to going home and taking a break from schoolwork. I wasn't looking forward to being away from Becky. I never knew that feeling of missing a girlfriend. It would be different. The second semester would be different, also.

Becky and I talked a couple of times over the break. She sent me a handmade card that was artfully done with a message that contained the words, "I love you." I was so happy and more eager than ever to see her again. I wasn't confused about how I felt for her, but I also had reservations about saying I loved her. Not because I didn't, but because it meant so much to me to say that to someone. In my mind, those words came with an understanding that I wasn't sure we both considered. At some point, we had to make life decisions that could alter our plans before we knew each other. I was more concerned for her than I was for myself. I had no long-term plans. I landed at Viterbo and in Theater Arts almost by default. She had her future in theater all planned out. I was trying to figure out who I was and what I should really do with the rest of my life.

When we saw each other for the first time back at school, she brought me some Christmas presents. She had a nice denim vest, a plaid shirt to wear with it, and a gold necklace with what she told me was an "Italian Love Horn" on it. These items looked like they cost some real money. I was overwhelmed and embarrassed because I didn't buy her anything. I promised to put the necklace on and never take it off. We picked up our routine again, right where we left off. We were getting closer, and I was glad.

I was waiting for David to return as well, so we could catch up on our happenings and I could show him my Christmas presents. It just so happened that David had some news as well when he returned to school. In our usual nightly gab session, he confessed that he would ask Rose to marry him. They couldn't stand to be apart from each other, and it was getting harder to do schoolwork and go home every weekend to see her. It sounded like she would be coming to La Crosse next year, and they would live together. I showed him my "Love Horn," and he had a great time teasing me about its secret powers.

As David was leaving most weekends, I decided I needed to find other friends to hang out with. I had started spending more time in the green room, and there were a couple of theater majors that I enjoyed bantering with. One was Hap Turner. He was a sophomore from La Farge, WI. Hap was the king of insincerity. He could speak to anyone with a keen interest and immediately roll his eyes as they walked away. Hap was medium height and build. He had an olive complexion, dark eyes, straight dark hair with a "Hitler" middle part, and a dark oversized "Hitler" mustache. His appearance was such that he could pass for Hispanic, Asian, Slavic, or many other ethnic backgrounds.

I found him funny because of his cutting sarcasm and deliberate phony portrayals. That is to say that Hap was a bullshitter of the highest order.

Another fellow I found pretty interesting and related to quite well was Jeff Luchsinger, a junior from Janesville, WI. Jeff was known as the old man, being 26 years old. He was a petite, wiry guy with long hair and a beard like Dan Fogelberg or Bob Seger. He smoked Marlboros and played his 12-string guitar. Unlike most other theater majors, he was quiet most of the time and didn't perform constantly. He chose his words carefully and had a great dry sense of humor that he shared at just the right moment. He and I both loved Steve Martin and enjoyed making "Wild and Crazy Guy" references to each other.

It was through Hap and Jeff that I met with another guy on campus, Wes Clark. What was so ironic is that I had known Wes in high school as he was a senior when I was a sophomore. Wes was from Black River Falls, WI, and lived in Apt. 6 down at the West end of the first-floor hallway. Wes was studying history and had a work-study job in the cafeteria, keeping him busy when not in class. Through Jeff and Hap, Wes and I became reacquainted, so I was invited to his apartment to hang out and partake in "Wes's World."

Wes was of average height and build with wispy blond hair, a receding hairline with a pronounced widow's peak, a round nose, expressive eyes, and a deviant smile. He also had an unkempt thin mustache that he often twisted on one side nervously in a Snidely Whiplash fashion. Wes was the most outspoken person I had ever met. He said whatever he was thinking to anyone without regard to consequence. If he thought you were a saint or an asshole, it didn't matter; he would say it to your face. I kind of admired that quality in him. It didn't bother me because he was willing to be judged similarly. He also had a hilarious nickname, "Snark." How he acquired the name was never really explained, but the popular belief was that some drunk or stoned partygoer somehow combined shark and narc and liked that it rhymed with Clark. So most who knew Wes well called him Snark.

Wes loved to host parties in his apartment and was very careful to invite a few close male friends and a larger number of females that he found attractive. Wes prided himself on his choice of beverages, like Frasier Crane, many times having more than one beer option. He often pointed out that the cheap bastards would only have "Old Style" or "Blatz," and he spent the extra on "Special Export" or "Heineken," the beers of the cultured in the world. He also ensured that anyone who entered coughed up some cash to help pay for the refreshments. His parties were an authentic experience in comparison to the standard beer bash. Wes always played the alternative radio station to "Top 40." We would listen to album cuts from Todd Rundgren, Gino Vannelli, The Marshall Tucker Band, or Neil Young. He had a large padlocked wooden box that served as his coffee table and contained a collector's quality selection of Playboy Magazine, saved from several years. No one but his closest confidants was allowed to view these treasures. He often bragged like an art collector of his treasures and ensured that all girls at his party knew about them even though they weren't allowed to see them.

Wes's parties usually ended when Wes would ask just about everyone to leave. Once most had gone, he would break out his pot stash, put wet towels under the entry door, close all the curtains, light up, and pass the joint or pipe around. Everyone did not need to partake, but Wes preferred that those not interested go home. I have to say I left at that point as I had no interest in the use or the chance of getting caught. I didn't care if people used it or not. Most of us were pretty drunk by then, anyway. I also knew that Becky had a natural aversion to the idea and wasn't a fan of Wes either. I don't know precisely why I became close friends with Wes, but there was a part of him that I found funny, honest, and different from others. He also told me that he had just broken up with his high school sweetheart, and I could tell he was genuinely hurt. I knew about being hurt.

Wes loved to have political or philosophical discussions. He shared that his father had died young, and he adored his mother. A quality I could relate to. He admired women and was unafraid to talk to them about anything from college and relationships to sex. I will never know how he got away with it, but more than a few girls seemed happy to oblige. It might be worth noting that Viterbo College in 1977 comprised about 1000 students. More than 900 were female. Considering that most of the girls were full-fledged Catholics and the apples of their daddy's eyes, it might explain their curiosity. The 100 or so men on campus, of which I could be counted, weren't exactly the cream of the crop either. If I had to estimate, at least 20 were gays or not interested in females, with the rest being a mix of music majors, theology students, nursing students, and the lost, like me. Not a ton of athletes in the group either, as it was a struggle to field the 76er's basketball team. There were some excellent basketball players in the group and, indeed, 2 or 3 tall, handsome strangers on campus, but the fact that I, Wes, or Hap, might be in the top ten most eligible bachelors wouldn't help the college recruiting brochures. I also discovered that many males in the Theater Department were "gay," as the term was used back then. Speaking of that, I was dismayed but not surprised to learn that Father Recker had been suspected of homosexual philandering in his past. This got him in trouble with the church leadership, forcing him to Viterbo to be away from younger men. Gossip in the department suggested that current students spent evenings at Father's residence occasionally. I didn't participate in those discussions, but I was glad Father never made advances in my direction or displayed his tendencies in classes or rehearsals. I never disclosed these things to my parents, as it would be impossible to explain. I was thankful that Becky had come into my world and that La Crosse was home to the "World's Largest Six Pack."

Chapter Five:

First Love

Before I realized it, the year was winding down, and so many things had changed since I started. David confided in me that Rose was pregnant and they had plans for a summer wedding. He asked if I would stand beside him as a groomsman. I said absolutely and was honored to be asked. It also meant that David would not be living in the dorms next year. Hap, Jeff, Wes, and I decided that we should join forces next year, so at least I won't have to look for a roommate.

Becky's birthday came in April. I bought her a cameo necklace, and we celebrated by going to dinner at Michael's Cerise Club in La Crosse. She loved the necklace and the new car her parents gave her. It was a little red Buick Opel, a 4-door and 4-speed sedan with a black leather interior and black striping. She had told me her family had some money because her father managed a couple of banks, but I was still surprised that they could afford to buy her a new car.

We both had landed parts in the last production of the year, "The Tempest." She had a substantial role as the spirit "Ariel." I was the "Boatswain" who initially appeared in the first scene and then went down with the ship. The way it staged out was that the boat was the orchestra pit that could be raised or lowered hydraulically. Since the story involved a shipwreck, down we went. Becky also told me she was going to be staying in La Crosse for summer school and auditioning for the summer repertory theater production. I couldn't afford summer school and needed to work in the summer to get my spending money for the next school year.

If there was any bright side to the coming summer, I knew we would be going to David's wedding together, and we had agreed that I would visit her at home in Chatfield during the Western Days Celebration. Before school ended, we did visit Black River one weekend, and Becky had a chance to meet my parents. My dad told all his regular stories, and she laughed in all the right places. My mother was thrilled I had met someone so adorable, and I could tell she liked Becky. We stayed overnight, and Becky slept in my sister's bedroom, and I was in my old bedroom. It was nice to wake up the next morning and see her immediately. We shared a good morning hug and kiss and then enjoyed my mother's breakfast before heading back to school. My mother made sure Becky knew she was welcome anytime.

Things were going well, and for the first time, I felt good about everything that had happened at school. I put to rest all the doubt about going to Viterbo, becoming a Theater Arts Major, and not having a more serious relationship with Kristen. The next big test would be getting through the summer and meeting Becky's parents.

That summer, my friend Ted and I worked for Ryan's dad at Strong Construction with the concrete crew. We were to be at the shop by 7:00 a.m. and then off to the job site with the rest of the team. I was surprised by how hard the work was. Everything was heavy and had bits of concrete crusted on it. I was in the hot sun for eight to ten hours every day. To the dismay of my red hair and fair skin, I was sunburned after the first two hours, and by the end of the day, my hands hurt so bad I could barely open them or make a fist. I also discovered that concrete has lye that loves to soak into every cut or scrape and sting like acid until you thoroughly wash it. I couldn't wait to get home, shower, and crawl into bed.

Jay Eddy

Every muscle in my body screamed at me the next morning as I got out of bed and headed back to work. It reminded me of the two-a-day football practices as a sophomore in high school. It would be a long summer at this rate, but I needed that $4.50 an hour. The majority of guys I worked with had been on the crew for a few years, and this was their livelihood. They had physically hardened like the concrete they poured.

Most evenings on the way home, the crew would hit the local watering hole, drink a few beers (or more), and continue their mindless conversations from the day. Outside of the details of the job tasks, most talks during the day consisted of sexual taunts about another worker's lack of penis size or someone's sexual fantasies about the perfect pussy or preference for the doggie style. It was ridiculously idiotic but, at the same time, entertaining. It certainly took my mind off the tediousness of the work. By the end of summer, I had learned how to contribute to the conversations and develop my construction worker appreciation for the female physique. In addition, I put on another 10 to 15 pounds of muscle, getting me up to my highest weight of about 185 pounds. I was grateful for that since I was the tall, skinny kid who could hide behind a telephone pole.

Becky and I exchanged a few phone calls and letters. We took her car to Mt. Hope for David and Rose's wedding in June. Driving down the highway was awesome, gazing at the scenery along the Mississippi, listening to Billy Joel's Stranger album on her cassette deck, and talking about school, family, and everything in between. I can't explain how easy it was to share how we felt about anything and everything for each other. Even when we disagreed on a topic, it never led to an argument. We often laughed, and she challenged me to change my ways or threatened half-heartedly to punish me somehow. I would then feign regret, beg for forgiveness, or ask for punishment with some kind of sexual innuendo.

Dave and Rose's ceremony included the typical Catholic Mass, and we couldn't help but be touched by how much they appeared to love each other. It's nothing like going to a friend's wedding to make a couple think more about their relationship. I know we danced a little closer than usual and held hands a little tighter afterward, neither of which bothered us in the slightest. I was really getting used to the idea of being referred to as a couple. Jay and Becky or Becky and Jay. One would always include the other. It was a powerful identifier for me, and I could start to understand all the relationships people sought in high school. I thought it shouldn't have had anything to do with ego, but the truth was that it did. I had overcome my self-doubt about being funny-looking and unattractive to women. Becky gave me so much confidence and genuine affection. I hated to say goodbye to her and go home again. We would see each other again for Western Days in August, and I was wishing my life away until then.

Life was pretty uneventful until one day, after work, I came into the house to find my mother staring at me in disgust and holding an envelope. I couldn't imagine what it might be. My mother asked what had been going on at college and then handed me the letter. It was unopened, so I looked at the exterior and saw it was from Hap. Written on the back of the envelope was a message to my mother, which said, "Mrs. Eddy, tell Jay to keep it in his pants." This would have made me laugh had I seen the letter first. I envisioned the smirk on Hap's face when he wrote it and the thrill he was taking in knowing I would be in hot water. I explained to my mother that it was Hap making a joke and that nothing was going on that she should be upset about. She told me there better not be, and maybe I should reconsider having Hap as my roommate next year. I apologized and told her it would never happen again.

I would deal with Hap the next time I saw him. The real purpose of the letter was to let me know our apartment number and when Jeff, Wes, and he were planning on moving in. True to form, they had planned a party that night, and I had to attend. I contemplated how to greet Hap that day. A rap upside his head or a swift kick in the nuts? Both seemed appropriate. Time will tell. August arrived and the event I was looking forward to all summer; Becky and I going to her house, meeting her parents, and taking in the "Western Days" celebration. We took her car (I still didn't own one) and headed west out of LaCrosse. It seems strange now, but at that time I had never been across the Mississippi into southern

Minnesota. On Interstate 90 we crossed the river and headed north with the bluffs on our left and the river on our right. I was mesmerized by the broad shimmering beauty of the Mississippi River and the seemingly endless backwaters stretching east into Lake Onalaska. A huge barge was working its way south and would soon be navigating another lock and dam on its long journey to New Orleans. Just past Dakota, MN, we turn westward and start to climb the 4-plus-mile Nodine hill. As we climb higher the valleys along the highway are deeper and darker and remind me of trips through the black hills as a kid. My ears start to pop as we crest the top and immediately the sky opens wide as we sit upon the plains of southern Minnesota. This country is wide open, and the interstate is a ribbon ahead of us as far as we can see, disappearing into the western horizon. The road winds slightly from north to south and back again. There are huge swaths of farmland and grass prairie dotted with the occasional farmhouse. Each house has the requisite white pine barrier on its north and west side, protecting it from the constant and unforgiving bitter winter winds. There are large silver grain bins looking like giant soup cans tucked next to the old red barns slumping on one side or another as years of driving rains cut away the soil and immense pressure from heaving frozen clay cracks their foundations. I find myself thinking of the courage of the early settlers deciding to stop out in this expanse; dreaming of the bountiful crops this land could produce but unaware of the ferocious, potentially deadly cold and snow coming shortly after harvest. As the signs for towns like Rushford and Houston pass by Becky gives me a primer on what to expect when we arrive at her house. Shortly we exit the interstate at St. Charles and head south and west on Hwy 74 toward Chatfield. The road meanders through the countryside slowly and gently dropping in elevation as we enter the Root River watershed. Our final turn takes us directly downward to the bottom of the valley and into the city. We pass by the town square, a charming little park with benches, monuments, and turn-of-the-century style lampposts. Then, turn onto River Dr., with mostly average homes with neatly groomed yards, some with white picket fences like you might see in a Norman Rockwell painting, and eventually to Becky's house. It is much larger than any of the homes we passed, and it features a large "U-shaped" entry driveway leading up to the front door. It's a big white two-story home with large white pillars on our front, and it is bigger than any house I have ever been invited too. We parked out front and went in through one of the double doors of the entry. We stop just inside as Becky tells me to wait here while she goes to tell her mother we are here. Before she can take a step, a booming female voice cascades from above, saying, "Becky, is that you." It is Becky's mom. Becky responds, "Yes, mother." Her mother says, "Is your friend with you?" Again, Becky responds, "Yes, Mother." Her mother then calls to her, "Come here." 'Okay," Becky replies and heads upstairs. I stay put and use the time to take in the wonder of the home I am seeing. Off of this huge circular formal entry, there are a number of entrances to other rooms. Becky is climbing the winding open staircase to the open balcony hallway of the second floor, and she disappears into the doorway to the right. The entry has white tile floors with white walls, and the staircase has white rails and red carpet. The wall along the staircase is covered with a fabric that is black with a silver foil inlay of some kind of design. To my right is an opening to what looks like a study, then another opening to a family room/den, then the entry to a formal dining room, which I can see just slightly. I notice a red carpet, a huge carved walnut dining room table with carved back walnut chairs with red velvet-covered seats that match the carpet. The final entry on the left goes down a hallway to what I assume must be the kitchen. As I am standing there, a lady appears out of the kitchen hallway and walks toward the den. She says "Hello" and keeps on going. I later learn that she is the maid. Becky came down the stairs with a broad smile and rolled her eyes as she told me we were to put our suitcases away and then head to the study to watch her sister Tammy's practice for her tap dance recital. I went out to the car and grabbed the bags following Becky upstairs to her room and then she showed me the guest room across the hall from hers. The guest room was huge with a queen size bed and bathroom with double vanity and shower. I had been in hotel rooms that weren't as nice. Together, we headed downstairs again and into the study. It was a nice size room with off-white walls covered in artwork. It had tracked lighting, a baby grand piano, and a fireplace that was two-sided with the other side being in the adjoining den. We sat down in a couple chairs and waited for Becky's mother and Tammy. Becky told me that this should be interesting and giggled at the thought of how her mother would expect us to be exceedingly complimentary of Tammy's efforts. Tammy came in and Becky went up to her and gave her a nice big sister hug and told how excited she was to see her dance. Tammy was about 8 years old, with curly brown hair, and still sporting some of her youthful baby weight. She had a huge smile on her face and was wearing some kind of costume dress and shiny black tap shoes. With her a lady who would be the piano accompanist came in and sat at the piano. Then Becky's mother entered the room. I stood up to greet her and she introduced herself, "I am Victoria Wise, Becky's mother." She was a shorter, somewhat stocky woman. She had on a dress, make-up, and a neatly styled wig, all of which looked very nice but I didn't expect as it was around 3:00 in the afternoon. She said, "Nice to meet you" as she gave me the once over. I could sense a small amount of dismay in her look; more than likely due to the fact the I was wearing an old pair of bib overalls, flannel shirt and hadn't had a haircut for a couple months. My mother would have been totally upset with me if she had known how I dressed to meet Becky's mom. We sat down and watched Tammy's performance and clapped loudly upon its completion as directed. Tammy loved it. Victoria then announced that Edward would be home at 4:00 for cocktails and then dinner would be served after. She suggested we might want to change for dinner beforehand. That was meant for me more than Becky but I had no problem with putting on something better to wear. Becky's mother excused herself and Tammy left with her. Becky and I visited for a moment and then I headed upstairs to put on the best clothes I had brought to wear which included the denim vest and plaid shirt Becky had given me for Christmas. I shaved, combed my hair, brushed my teeth, and then headed back downstairs. Becky gave me a tour of the rest of the house and told me in addition to having a maid, there was also a nanny that came for Tammy on the days that Victoria would have lunch dates or shopping trips with her friends. We waited in the den for Becky's dad to arrive. It was about 15 minutes later that a large green Lincoln Continental pulled into the garage, and someone entered through the kitchen. Victoria called from upstairs, "Edward, can you come up here please." Becky's dad then went upstairs carrying his briefcase. Just a few minutes later Victoria and Edward came down and entered the den. Becky's dad extended his hand and introduced himself in the same formal manner that Victoria did. Then he opened some bi-fold doors on one wall of the den and proceeded to pull out a bar. What would you like he asked everyone? While serving the drinks, he explained that he had designed the house himself and mentioned all the unique details, including the hidden roll out bar. I complimented him on how nice it all was and how it must have taken a great deal of planning. Becky's dad was an average-sized man with neatly groomed flat top hair, blond on the top with some gray on the sides. He was very demonstrative as he spoke, almost like a circus barker inviting the crowd to see one of the wonders of the world. He had me look through the large windows out to the back of the house and the yard and acreage he owned. In the distance he pointed out the north branch of the Root River. It was quietly moving like a shiny black snake warming itself in the afternoon sun. It reminded me of a large creek instead of a river but the amount of bottom land bordering it on both sides led me to belief it was prone to flooding in the spring or during large rains and could easily double or triple in size easily overflowing the sharp banks that held it now. We continued to visit as a group while Edward and Victoria had another martini, Becky still had her first beer and I was happy to have another old fashioned. I shared details of my family and few stories from my dad's repertoire that garnered the desired ice breaking laughter I was hoping for. The initial tensions seemed to subside and I felt very comfortable with Becky's parents and even noticed her mother smiling and seeing if she could get me to offer any other witticisms I might have. Soon the maid said dinner was ready and we took our places at the huge table in the dining room. We said the standard "Catholic Grace" and began the meal. It came in courses like at a restaurant which I had never experienced before. Becky's younger brother Eddie (Edward Jr.) sat to my right. He was in eighth grade and had an impish smile while he looked for my reaction to anything that was done or said. I got a kick out of him because I could remember my Junior High days and how I loved to cause a little trouble. I had the feeling that Eddie had his share of trips to the principal's office for clowning around in class. He also seemed naughtily pleased if he could get his mother to correct him while fighting to keep her composure. Becky confirmed later that Eddie was the character of the family and really a chip off the old Edward Wise Sr. block. The meal took about an hour and afterward Edward offered an after-dinner drink. Becky and I both declined and decided we would take a walk around town so she could show me the sights of Chatfield, MN. We got outside and Becky stopped to give me a kiss as if to say I passed the test of meeting her folks. Hand in hand we walked toward town and she pointed out different houses where her friends grew up. As we got closer to downtown, she showed me the auditorium where the Western Days production of "Showboat" was to take place Saturday night. The posters for the production were all over the town and each contained in large letters, "Directed by and Starring Dennis Wise." Becky's father and mother also had parts in the production to include a solo from Becky's mother. We stopped in the park of the town square sat on a bench and talked until the street lights came on. After a few minutes and a few kisses Becky decided we should head home before her mother went to bed. She would no doubt have to give her a report on my feelings about the day's happenings. I suggested she tell her I was disgusted with the whole thing. It was just after 10:00 when we got back. Becky told me to go the den and watch some tv if I wanted, and she went upstairs to talk to her mother. I went into the den and found her dad sitting watching the news. I sat with him and quietly watched while he would make a comment here and there about what was happening. The sports came on, and we talked about the "Twins" and the "Vikings," and he liked the idea that even thought I lived in Wisconsin, I held onto my Minnesota roots and team loyalties. Becky had returned and was in her pajamas. She said she was going to bed because it had been a long day, and tomorrow was going to be busy. She told her dad goodnight, and I said I would be heading to bed as well. We went upstairs and had one last quick kiss goodnight outside her bedroom door, and I headed into the guest room. I undressed and neatly folded my clothes, putting them on the dresser. I felt a little foolish for not packing some kind of robe or pajamas to wear for in the morning, but it wasn't part of my routine at home so I guessed I better get dressed in the morning before going down for breakfast. I crawled under the covers and enjoyed having such a large bed to sleep in. My feet didn't hang over the end like at home. I just laid there and replayed the day's events in my head until I finally dropped off to sleep. It couldn't have been very long but I was awakened by the voice of an angel whispering my name. Becky had snuck across the hall and into the room. I woke up and smiled. She said, "Are you ok." I said, "Ya just fine, how about you." She said, "just a little lonely." "Can I help" I asked in a rather phony innocent tone. We both snickered quietly and she crawled in the bed beside me. We held each other tightly and whispered sweet nothings back and forth for what seemed liked hours. After a long pause in the conversation, she turned away from me and then backed up into my body pulling my arm over her gripping it tightly across her chest. She closed her eyes and said "wake me up in a little while so I can go back to my room, ok?." "Ok" I said and lay still beside her. I had never felt so close to anyone other than my mother in my whole life. The warmth and the joy were almost overwhelming and I could feel tears of joy filling my eyes as I looked upon her sleeping beside me. I loved this girl and couldn't keep from thinking about how terrific the rest of our lives together would be. Maybe just maybe the story I had written for my life would have the happy ending of my dreams. Maybe.

Chapter Six:

The Bradford Incident

D ad dropped me off outside of Treacy House and headed home right away. As I went up the stairs toward Apartment 8 directly at the top, I could see the door was wide open, and I heard Marshall Tucker Band's "Can't You See" overpowering some conversation. I entered to find Jeff sitting on the loveseat, smoking a cigarette, and enjoying the music while Wes and Hap were talking to each other just outside the bedrooms.

"Hey Jaybird, what do you think?" asked Wes as he pointed to a massive set of Longhorns that he and Hap mounted above the side-by-side doorways to the bedrooms. "Well, the women should get the message if they see those," I said in my best nasty voice. We all laughed and then shook hands. Hap and I would share the room on the right, and Wes and Jeff, the "old men," would share the one on the left. Hap had decided that we should have our beds arranged in the bunk style, and he would take the top bunk. I agreed that would work, and it would be better for me as I couldn't hear him playing with himself during the night. He laughed, rolled his eyes, and then mimicked jacking off his imaginary giant member. That's when I confronted him about the message he wrote my mother in the letter he sent.

"Hap," I said, " If you ever pull some shit like that again, I will cut your balls and shove them down your throat. My mother was super pissed and didn't think it was funny at all."

"Oh man, I'm really sorry," he said in the phoniest academy award-winning regretful voice and then burst out in a belly laugh that nearly took his breath away.

"Hap, you're silly, fucker" Wes said. Jeff also joined in the laughter, setting the tone for communications in Apartment 8 for the rest of the year. There would be no real serious discussions without one roommate or another calling bullshit on each other.

I asked, "Wes, what time should the party start tonight?" Wes replied, "It's not going to happen tonight because there is a freshman mixer outside the pub at Marion Hall tonight, so we decided to crash that to get a look at the new crop of "Sweaty Bettys" coming in. Sweaty Bettys was the term we used for the overweight girls that we would watch make a second trip to the desert bar at the cafeteria in Marion Hall. Of course, we were looking for attractive girls to coax into coming to our dorm room parties during the year. "Wes likes meat with his potatoes," Hap commented.

"Hey Hap, fat girls need love too," Wes retorted. Again, all I could think was that we literally defined the word "Sophomoric."

I finished moving my stuff in and put my 19" color TV on the stand in the left corner of the living room. The right corner of the room had a massive trunk that Wes had brought from his mother's farmhouse. At the top of his setup was his sound system. It featured a "Marantz" receiver, boasting 40 watts per channel and equipped with a built-in dual cassette tape deck. Adjacent to it was a "Pioneer" turntable, and a "Marantz" graphic equalizer. On either side of the floor in the trunk area, there were "Bose" 501 speakers, complete with the remarkable "Bose Woofer" along with mid-range and tweeters. Wes was very proud of this system, which represented a healthy investment then. The speakers alone were almost $500.00.

All of these were purchased from the legendary "Hi-Fi" Kenny, who traveled to Wisconsin and advertised blowout sales on stereo equipment that he would sell directly out of the back of a truck at a local auditorium or in a stereo store parking lot. Wes had laid down the law that "any of you stupid fuckers blow out those speakers, and you are going to pay for them." Therefore, everyone was careful to get his permission to play their music or turn up the volume.

Above the stereo system and hanging from the walls and ceiling was some fishnet one might use to catch minnows in a stream. Strung in the fish net were colorful "Christmas Lights" that Wes felt would add some ambiance, encouraging female guests to relax during some hopeful, intimate visit. Eventually, we would add a couple of neon beer signs borrowed from the "Wunderbar" without their knowledge.

One a "Blatz" and the other a "Special Export" to class up the joint. Wes had other rules he laid out during the year, like when the door was shut and a sock hanging on the knob meant keeping out.

Hap and I ignored most of them, and Jeff wasn't subject to any of them being the elder statesman. Nearly every night at bedtime, once the lights were out, Hap began his goodnights to everyone like the Walton children had done on TV. True to form, however, no one had regular names like "John Boy." Wes was "Snark" or "Pussy Fart" or whatever ridiculous name Hap could use. Wes would have to return with an equally offensive reply like "Good night, penis breath."

We would all laugh out loud and eventually tire of the nonsense and go to sleep. Higher education would take a strange path at this "Catholic Affiliated Co-Educational Christian Liberal Arts College."

I was thrilled to find out that Father Recker had arranged for my work-study job to be in the scene shop of the fine arts center. Theater students could be paid for helping construct sets, do lighting, paint, and other technical tasks required for play productions. Most of the hours were during the daytime and included Saturday mornings. That meant I could work between classes, and my nights would be free for study, rehearsals, or any other activity I could fit in.

Surviving Myself

Tom Schunk was the technical director for the theater department and supervised the scene shop. Tom was a great teacher also. He was a Vietnam Vet who got a college degree on the GI bill after coming home. Tom had slick-backed black hair, a beard, and a mustache with a few gray hair. He wore wire-rimmed glasses, traditional straight-leg blue jeans and a wide leather belt adorned with a large ornate silver belt buckle. In his shirt pocket was always a pack of Camel Straight cigarettes, and I don't think I ever saw him without a cup of coffee or smoke in his hand.

Tom was a friendly fellow who had all kinds of patience when instructing but was very adamant about the cleanliness and organization of his shop. I could tell the military had taught him the value of a place for everything and everything in its place. The faculty of Viterbo College at that time consisted of an equal amount of laypeople and Catholic Nuns. The nuns belonged to the Franciscan Sisters of Perpetual Adoration and the St. Rose Convent. Most nuns lived on campus right next to the main building.

These sisters' claim to fame was that they had been praying for our world non-stop, 24 hours a day, and seven days a week, in their adoration chapel for some 100 years. They also donated approximately two million dollars to the college to build the Fine Arts Center.

I didn't know much about Catholicism, but I was impressed with the devotion of these ladies. Most of these sisters were elderly. I had Sr. Marie Leon for many theater arts subjects, Sr. Bernine for French, Sr. Celestine for Shakespeare, Sr. Arita for Wisdom and Old Testament Writings, and Sr. Mary Conrad Krause for Comp and Lit, especially Oriental Literature.

All of these sisters were very sharp and had the patience of the saints. The youngest of these nuns was Sister Mary Conrad. She looked to be in her mid-30s and was a beautiful woman. She was thin with a nice figure, wore high-heeled shoes and nylons, and had her hair styled in the mode of the day. She reminded me of Mary Tyler Moore in both appearance and character. We had a few discussions, and I asked her about her life before becoming a nun. She said she had not led a Christian life and had done things that she regretted but thanked God for His forgiveness and saving grace. She was an incredible woman with a great vibe. All the kids adored her; I thought she would have made someone a great wife.

Becky had moved off campus and into an apartment with three other girls from the theater department. There was Lynne Vosen, who grew up knowing Hap in LaFarge, and Kim Little, a farm girl from somewhere in Iowa. She was very interested in becoming a costume designer and would succeed eventually, having her own company in Los Angeles and getting an Academy Award for work on costumes for the Star Trek movie.

They were all pleasant, friendly people who wanted to make it in the theater. Becky fit right in with this group and liked the independence of off-campus life because I didn't have to check in at the front desk to see her.

This was going to be a busy year for me in the Theater Department. I landed a role right away in The Importance of Being Earnest, an Oscar Wilde classic. I was the Reverend Cannon Chasuble—it was not a huge role, but it was larger than anything I had previously played. With rehearsals, doing set construction, and helping with the lighting design, it kept me busy until 9 or 10 p.m. most nights. That cut in on Becky and I having much time outside of seeing each other during shared classes each day. We changed our date night to Saturday night as it was the only night (outside of performances) that something theater wasn't going on. On one of the balmy Saturday afternoons, Becky and I often went to Riverside or Pettibone Park along the Mississippi with a blanket, cooler, and radio. It was a chance to be away from all the noise of the people and the "drama" of the theater department.

One Saturday night, she even took me to The Guthrie Theater in Minneapolis to take in "Hamlet." It was the best play I had ever been to, and I will never forget the lead actor, Randall Duk Kim. His curtain call alone was among the most exciting things I had ever seen. The audience came to their feet cheering, and he guided their cheers like an orchestra conductor. Waiving his harm, kneeling, or simultaneously raising both arms causes the crowd to roar even louder. It inspired me to develop a routine I called the "Curtain Call." I would ask the department to participate by applauding and then trying to guess what kind of actor I was portraying simply by observing my curtain call.

It was fun, and everyone enjoyed it. Father Recker would fall on the floor laughing. He especially liked the first-time curtain call actor, and the actor was upset they didn't get the lead. If you have never been in the theater or never participated in a curtain call, you might not get it, but those who have understood it well.

One Saturday afternoon, I called Becky to see what she wanted to do that night. She said she couldn't go out as she had made other plans. Jim Bradford, a junior music major, had asked her to attend the orchestra concert in the music recital hall. I said, "What?" There was silence, and then almost immediately, I felt my heart rate increase, my entire body shake, my face get hot, and my voice became strident and uncontrollable.

Totally enraged and without a second thought, I screamed into the phone, "Well, Jim Bradford is a dead man! I am going to kill that son-of-a bitch," and I slammed down the phone receiver. Wes and Hap heard the commotion, and Hap said, "What the fuck was that about, dude?" I told him, still screaming as I talked and spit coming out of the corner of my mouth, "Fucking Jim Bradford asked Becky out tonight, and I am going to kill that motherfucker." I left the apartment and headed down the hall to apartment 12, where I knew Jim Bradford lived. I knocked, didn't wait for a response, and then rushed in. Jim was sitting in a chair in the corner of the room, talking on the telephone. He saw me, and the look in his eyes was sheer terror. I went to him, grabbed the receiver of the phone out of his hand, and then grabbed him by the hair on the top of his head and slammed his head against the wood rail on the back of the chair, pinning it there while I said, "Who the fuck do you think you are asking Becky out for a date? I'm gonna bash your goddamn brains out." I then grabbed the phone and pressed the receiver tight against his temple, grinding it into his head, fully intending to pound him to death. He didn't or couldn't resist me, but he hollered in a scared voice, "She never said you guys were going out together; I didn't know!" I could tell he wasn't lying. I paused for a second from my tirade and released his head. "Well, I'm telling you now, and if I ever see you talking to her or even see you on the same side of the street, I will fucking kill you, got it?"

I stormed out without closing the door and headed back to my apartment. Hap and Wes were hanging out in the hallway, trying to catch a glimpse into Bradford's apartment, hoping to see a dead body. Wes said, "So, did you kill that fucking faggot."

I replied, "He told me Becky didn't tell him we were a couple and dating." I was still shaking and exceedingly loud as I spoke; Hap said, "What?" That bitch didn't say anything?" I said, "Shut the fuck up, Hap. I'm not in the mood." Hap backed away from me as if he thought I might punch him. "Okay, easy, man," he said. I then went into my bedroom, collected everything Becky had ever given me, including clothes, the Italian Love Horn, and all the cards and letters we had exchanged, and put them in a paper bag. I then left the apartment and headed to Becky's.

It was about a three-block walk, and I was fuming nearly the entire time. My mind was racing, trying to figure out what to say and what I had done that she would consider going out with someone else. I went into her building and upstairs to her apartment on the second floor. I pounded on the door loud enough to wake the dead. Lynne answered and peeked through the tiny crack, keeping the opening as small as possible.

I said, "Is Becky here?" Lynne responded in a guarded tone, "Yes, but she isn't going to come to the door." Apparently, someone had called ahead to make them aware I was on the way and what my state of mind was at the time. "Well, then, could you do me a favor?' I said somewhat sarcastically, "Give her this," extending the bag out, "And tell her if we aren't a couple, I don't need any of this shit reminding me of her!" I dropped the bag and left. Once outside, my anger gave way to sadness. My body was exhausted and needed some way to unload all the adrenaline it had produced. I walked around town for the next hour or more, fighting back sobs and trying to gather myself before returning to my apartment.

I was hurt, embarrassed, and ashamed all at the same time. I had never been that angry that quickly since I was a small kid being tormented by my older brothers. I literally had no control over it. Why Jim Bradford, I thought. Jim Bradford was a blond-haired, blue-eyed, nice-looking kid from LaCrosse. I assumed he was homosexual. He was always nicely dressed with a tie, sweater vest, and corduroy slacks. He often wore a long black wool coat that probably cost a couple hundred bucks.

He had thick black horn-rimmed glasses, and I remember thinking what a fucking "Poindexter" he looked like. He was an only child, and his parents had money, and I think that was something Becky saw in him. I figured that people with money must be fully aware of others who are in their economic class. He also liked music and played many instruments, which Becky would find interesting. She played the French Horn and probably had participated in and attended orchestra concerts in the past. It was going to take me a long time to process. In the meantime, the funny makes everyone laugh. Jay was going to be a thing of the past. I was tired of not being taken seriously and being the one who everyone, especially women, could shit on.

Word of the "Bradford Incident" spread quickly around campus, especially in the theater department. A few days later, when I entered the green room, it was like I had a contagious disease. People moved away and gave me plenty of room. I wasn't mean to anyone, but I didn't perform for the group like I had in the past. I took the opportunity to seek more "therapy" at Wunderbar. Over this time, Becky and I exchanged glances daily, and I could tell she was also hurting. I just couldn't be the one to start any conversation. I had very little self-esteem left, and my pride prevented me from giving in.

If there were to be some kind of reconciliation for us, it would have to come from her or God. I don't think God was holding any services at Wunderbar.

When Saturday came around again, Becky called me and asked if she could talk to me. I said yes, and she came over to Treacy House. We went downstairs to the rec room, usually empty on Saturday mornings, and sat on the couch. She was shaking, and her voice quivered as she said she was sorry for what happened. Tears came to her eyes, and she said, "You know I love you, right?" I hadn't seen her cry ever. It was hard for me to see. "I know," I said, and you know I love you, too."

"I'm sorry I got so upset, but I don't understand why you wanted to go out with Jim Bradford?" I inquired.

She then explained that she had no feelings for Jim Bradford and wanted to attend the orchestra concert. She didn't think I would like to go—which was correct—and she would only go with Jim as a friend. She wanted to say that on our phone call that day, but I didn't give her a chance. She grabbed my hand, leaned in, and kissed me. "Listen," I said, "I haven't had much luck with relationships until I met you. If it weren't for you, I might not have stayed here in the theater department." I went on to tell her how profound my feelings were for her and that I never wanted to lose her. "You're not going to lose me," she said in her pretend stern voice she often used to make me laugh. So, we touched foreheads and looked into each other's eyes like we had many times before. "I guess I should tell Jim Bradford I'm sorry so he doesn't shit his pants if we meet on the street then," I said. "That's up to you," she said. "And tell your roommates I'm not mad at any of them," I instructed. "I don't want them to think I am some kind of psycho." "They were surprised that you had that side to you," she said. "Let's just do our best to move on and not repeat this," I said. "Okay," she replied. So we hugged, kissed, and talked about our usual things like theater classes and our families. A huge weight had been removed from my heart, and we would grow deeper together as time passed. Our parents would later meet each other, and we all went to dinner together. It was a great night of laughs and really felt like an affirmation of our relationship. Then it was my turn.…. "

One evening, David got up from his bed and strolled around on the roof of the palace." - Holy Bible 2 Samuel, verse 11-2a.

Chapter Seven:

Indiscretion

Father Recker made an exciting announcement that Viterbo had been awarded the honor of the Midwest Host Site for the Midwest Finals Competition of The American College Theater Festival. This competition among participating colleges would be judged by an independent council, with the winner getting the opportunity to go to Washington, D. C., and perform at the Kennedy Arts Center. It meant we would have a production enter the competition and be quite busy for the next 8-10 weeks getting ready for the finals. Six schools would be coming to Viterbo to perform their productions in hopes of being chosen. Father had entered Viterbo into the competition for the first time. He had chosen a play called "The Shadow Box," which had won the 1977 Tony Award for drama. It has four female and five male parts, all considered leads. Whoever got cast in the show would be professionally critiqued and have the chance to perform in front of a distinguished audience if we made it to D.C.

Everyone in the department was excited and hopeful to land a role. The Shadow Box is the story of three people, Joe, Brian, and Felicity, who are dying of terminal cancer and agree to spend their final days at a research facility where the family dynamics surrounding a terminal illness can be studied and recorded. Intense and emotional. It would challenge all of us who spent most of our acting careers in musicals or lighthearted farcical comedies written for the high school stage and audience.

I had my best audition ever and, along with Jeff, was in the running for the part of Joe. Becky also had a terrific audition, and I was sure she would land the role of Felicity or Agnes, the daughter of Felicity. This is where I learned that the "Theater" and life share some brutal truths. You may be the best at something, but it doesn't mean you will play the part.

The casting director has the final say about selection and their opinion counts. Just like the business owner can pick who they want for promotion regardless of performance. In professional theater, it isn't only how well you can act but also what you look like. What you look like might be more critical. Jeff got the role of Joe not because his audition was better than mine but because Jeff looked like an older man. He was slight of frame and had sunken cheeks and tired eyes.

I was 6'2 and 185 pounds with bright red hair and a rosy complexion. I did get an equally important role of "The Interviewer."

This character, however, did not appear on stage but only spoke through a speaker to each character. Father told me that I was the only one he felt had the vocal ability to carry off this part. The Interviewer is part of nearly every scene and is the physician dealing with each patient. He develops a personal/professional relationship with each character and often hears confessions from their lives. It symbolically feels as if they are talking to God. It was a great challenge and my most exciting role ever. Becky did not get either part she wanted. Again, it had nothing to do with her audition but everything to do with how the girls who got those parts looked.

The girl who got Felicity was a tall, thin freshman with a very pointed nose, big sunken eyes, wild hair, and a strange voice. It was not a stretch to think of her as an older woman. Mary Hare got the part of Agnes. Mary always looked scared with those big eyes and pale complexion. Her voice had just a little hint of shakiness, too. Becky was noticeably upset, and for the first time, she showed a side to her that I hadn't noticed before.

She had an ego when it came to her acting ability. She was especially discouraged because she wanted to participate in the festival and be critiqued by professional theater people. She didn't show her true feelings to anyone else, but privately, she told me she wasn't thrilled with Father Recker and his abilities. I did what I could to help her overcome it, but I also had to live up to the adage that the show must go on.

Wes and Hap went downtown on Thursday nights as that had become the real party night in LaCrosse. The reason was that many kids went home for the weekends on Friday nights from UW-LaCrosse, Western Tech, and Viterbo. So, if you were looking forward to seeing the most women, Thursday night was the time to go. When I could, I would go with them. I did enjoy the crowds of kids and got plenty of laughs watching Wes and Hap strike out with the co-eds. My favorite bar was "The Time Square." They had a great house band called "The Changing Times," who could cover nearly every hit song. The place boasted a modest dance floor, where the girls couldn't resist but to go out and "shake their groove thing." Back in the day, the legal drinking age was 18. It was a simple rule of thumb: if you were old enough to get "Drafted and Shafted," you were certainly old enough to get "Loose on the Juice."

Third Street in LaCrosse was famous for its bars back then. From King Street to Vine Street, there were three to four bars/taverns per block on both sides of the street. The places we haunted most were Popcorn Tavern, Golden Garter, Times Square, and Del's Bar. We also regrettably one night visited "The Blue Tiger."

This was the only strip club downtown, and Wes was fascinated with the idea of going there because he heard the girls were black. We entered that night with a snoot, having hit all the regular spots beforehand. The smell of what must have been used gym socks mixed with a burning bale of marijuana hit me immediately. I kind of choked a little as we made our way through the haze, trying to find a table with only the light being the dull blue neon lights of the small stage.

We sat down not far from the door as we felt we might need to leave immediately. Soon, a tall, thin, topless, black woman who looked about 40 years old sauntered to our table. She asked what we wanted to drink in a slow, drawn-out voice like she was stoned. We said a round of tap beers. She then leaned over the table toward Wes in the most raspy voice and said, "Do you have any smoke, baby?"

Wes leaned back and said rather dumbly, "No, we don't smoke." She smiled and headed toward the bar for our beers. She returned with a tray and said, "That'll be 15 dollars."

We looked at each other, thinking she must be mistaken. Three tap beers for 15 dollars?

"We just ordered beers," Wes said, "Are you sure it's 15 dollars?"

"Oh yes, honey," she laughed, "It includes the show." About that time, an even skinnier and more stoned black girl got up on the stage, turned on a boom box with some hip music, and began dancing and removing the few items of clothing she was wearing.

I looked at my glass of beer and noticed the head had already gone flat. That usually indicated either stale beer or a dirty glass.

"I've seen enough," I said, heading for the door. "Wait! Wes said," You have to finish your beer." "Go Ahead," I said and left. That would be the last time I ventured into The Blue Tiger.

It wasn't unusual for us to leave our apartment door open when we were home. It made it easy for kids to come in, and we didn't always have to get up to answer the door.

One Friday night, we went to Wunderbar for happy hour and made the fish fry at the cafeteria before it closed. Wes and Hap wanted to hit Schmitty's bar after and then go downtown. I said I was going home to watch some TV for a while, and they could get me before going downtown. Becky was going home for the weekend, so I knew I had plenty of time to finish drinking. So I went to the apartment, left the door open just in case, and laid down on the couch to watch TV. I either fell asleep or passed out, whichever didn't matter. I have no idea how long I had been out, but I awoke and had the strange feeling that I was being watched.

As I sat up, a gorgeous blonde-haired, bare-footed girl sat in the chair, drinking a beer. I told her, "If you're looking for Wes and Hap, I don't think they are here."

She replied, "I know; I wasn't looking for them." "You talked to them," I asked. "Yes, they told me you would be here," she said. "Oh," I said, confused. She told me her name was Tina, and she went to Viterbo in nursing. And she had heard some girls on 3 South talk about me in their lounge one night. Marion Hall was the girls' dorm, and they had the south wing and the north wing with the traditional two-person 10'x10' dormitory-style rooms with community bathrooms on each floor and TV lounges at the end of the halls. She then said she had seen me at the Popcorn Tavern last week and wanted to talk to me then, but there were so many kids around that she couldn't get to me before we left. "Do you need another beer?" I asked. "I'm going to get myself one." "Sure," she said. I went to the fridge, grabbed a couple of cold ones, and returned to the couch to sit down. She then asked, "Care if I sit by you?" Without thinking, I said, "I don't care."

She made her way over to the couch and sat down uncomfortably close to me. In the back of my mind, I started thinking that Wes and Hap sent her to the room for some joke. It was precisely the kind of humor Hap would find amusing.

I couldn't help myself, so I had to ask, "Did Wes or Hap ask you to come up here?" "No," she said. "Why," she asked. I explained that I didn't understand why she was there and thought maybe it was one of their practical jokes. She told me she just wanted to meet me, and it had nothing to do with Wes or Hap.

We shared some small talk for a few minutes. Then, out of the blue, she asked, "Can I kiss you." My response should have been no! But

Tina was beautiful. She was built like the proverbial "brick shit house," had gem-quality emerald green eyes, a perfect complexion, unnaturally white teeth of professional proportion, and an intensity to her glance that would back down a grizzly.

"Sure," I said, expecting a soft, quiet initial introductory type of kiss. Instead, she pressed into me with her solid body, pinning me to the back of the couch and giving me a full open-mouth kiss, driving her tongue to the back of my mouth as if to check if I had swollen glands. Being a man, I was compelled to respond in kind, and we made out like crazy people for the next 15 to 20 minutes.

She bit my bottom lip at one point, and I could taste blood in my mouth. She paused momentarily and said, "Sorry," half smiling like she had gotten away with something. Then she reached up on my shirt and began stroking my chest. I attempted to do the same, and she made a slight whimpering "No" request.

So I stopped, and we continued our wrestling match. I couldn't help but think back to Beth and the bus. After another couple of minutes, I pulled back and said we should stop before Wes and Hap got back. Then she said, "Can you do some theater for me?"

"What do you mean?" I asked" "You know," she said, "Act out something." I didn't have anything I could do, so I said I could read some Shakespeare from my Riverside Shakespeare Book in my bedroom. "Cool," she gleefully cheered. We entered my bedroom, and I told her to sit on Hap' top bunk. Then I grabbed my Shakespeare book and read to her the balcony scene from Romeo and Juliet with my best Richard Burton English accent. "But soft, what light through yonder window breaks, it is the East, and Juliet is the Sun."

She was enthralled and looked at me like I had just asked her to marry me. I finished, and she jumped down and gave me another heart-starting kiss. We could hear Wes and Hap entering the building at the bottom of the stairs. "You better go," I said. "Okay," she said and took off out of the apartment and down the stairs, passing Wes and Hap on the way down. I returned to the living room to figure out what had just happened. Wes and Hap came in and wanted to know if she had been there. I asked, "Did you guys send her here?"

Hap said, "Yeah, we ran into her leaving Marion Hall, and she asked where you were, so we told her." "Well, I was sleeping, and when I woke up, she was sitting here drinking a beer," I said. "Before I knew it, she wanted to sit by me and then started kissing me like a crazy person," I continued. "I thought it was set up." "No shit," Wes said. "So what happened next, you old stud?" he joked. I explained the make-out session, her biting my lip and ending with the Shakespeare reading. Hap laughed, "So Romeo, did you fuck Juliet?"

"No," I said.

"She is so damn hot," Hap said. I told Wes and Hap not to say anything to anybody because I didn't want Becky to find out. I also told them she was strange because she tried to kiss me like a madwoman but didn't want me to touch her anywhere. Maybe she was just drunk and looking for some companionship. I don't know. I figured that I wouldn't see her again anyway.

The next day, Hap returned from Marion Hall and said there was a message for me on the student message board in the Marion Hall student lounge. I walked over, and sure enough, there pinned to the board was a small note on notebook paper, folded in a square and stapled on the corners, with my name on it. I took it down and opened it.

It was from Tina, and she wanted to see me again. I put it in my pocket and headed down the back hallway to the east exit doors below the cafeteria to leave. As I approached the end of the hallway and walked through the small hidden alcove, someone jumped out onto my back. It was Tina, and she put her arms around my neck and hung on piggyback style while kissing and biting at my ears. "What are you doing?" I exclaimed.

She giggled and said, "I wanted to surprise you," she said. "Well, you did," I answered. She got down, and I turned around so we were face to face. She flung her arms around my neck and started kissing me again. "Tina," I said rather firmly, we need to talk. We returned to the student lounge and into the TV room off the main room. It was about a 10 x 10 room with orange shag carpeted walls and carpeted built-in bench for sitting that went ¾ around the room.

One wall had the TV in a recessed cabinet. No one was in the room, and the carpet made it so sound didn't travel outside the room. We sat in there and talked about what we were doing. She said she liked me and just wanted to spend time with me. I wasn't sure what to say to her. I would be lying if I didn't say I enjoyed her physical contact, but I couldn't have her jumping on me publicly. I explained to her that if we were to see each other, it would have to be in my apartment and no other place. We could see each other in other places if things worked out, but we needed to take our time. She was fine with that. Once I thought we had an understanding, we went right back to our make-out session. I was playing with fire, and I knew it.

There was something addictive about Tina, and I was hooked. It wasn't just her "hotness" but the fact that she chose me. My ego had swelled as much as other parts of my body. Like any addict, I was sure I could control it and hide it from anyone until I figured out what else to do. Over the next week, she would come to the apartment around 10:30 at night. She would come in, and we would exchange a few words, getting to know each other more and more, and then right back to the exercise.

Each night, she was more willing to allow me to touch her body, outside her clothes initially and then carefully under them as time passed. I wasn't disappointed with what I found. The more I experienced, the more I wanted. Now, I was the one willing to take more chances. I had been burning the candle at both ends and was about to find out why that cautionary cliché became famous. I had lied to Becky several times during the week about staying late at the Fine Arts Center to prepare for the festival. She took me at my word, and why wouldn't she? I hadn't lied to her before. Friday night came, and I did work late at the fine arts center because I knew I wouldn't be working on Saturday.

As I got back to my apartment, Tina was waiting for me. Wes and Hap weren't there, and neither was Jeff. I came in and grabbed a beer out of the fridge. I sat on the couch, and Tina took her spot next to me. We talked for a while, and I told her I was super tired as it had been a long week, and I planned on going to bed when I finished my beer.

Surprisingly, she said, "I want to stay with you tonight." I took a big swig of my beer, and after thinking for a minute, I said, "Okay."

She snuggled into me while I finished my beer and didn't say anything. I got up, and she held my hand while I guided her into the bedroom. I closed the door behind her and reached to turn the light on. She asked me to leave the light off. We then stood next to the bunk and embraced each other. After a few kisses, she backed away slightly and started removing her clothes. I did the same, keeping my eyes on her the whole time. The only light was the green glow of the time display on Hap' digital alarm radio on the dresser. It was enough for me to see her naked in front of me.

She was more beautiful than any woman I had ever seen. I was totally naked as well, and I assumed we would fall into bed and make love. We got under the covers and pressed against each other face to face without any space in between our bodies. We began kissing. I was fully prepared in every way to roll on top of her to consummate this relationship. She stopped kissing me as I moved into position and said, "I don't want to do that. I just want to feel you close to me."

I laid back down flat again, complying with her wishes. I waited for her to make the next move. My mind agreed with her, but my body remained at attention in case there was a change in her intent. She rolled away from me onto her side and slid her backside into my body, pressing against my genitals while grabbing my left arm and wrapping it around her. She closed her eyes and said, "Goodnight." I lay there in perpetual arousal, my heart pounding and my eyes fixated on her face. My thoughts were all over the place.

Part of me wondered what was going through this girl's mind. She was physically intense but didn't want the total intimacy of lovemaking.

Was that normal? How could I know? The only girl I had made love to was , and there was no hesitation with her. The only girl I wanted to make love to was Becky, and I knew that wasn't going to happen until we were married. I closed my eyes and tried to ignore the signals my body was sending to my brain. Eventually, I fell asleep.

Hap jumping down from his bunk above awakened me the next morning. He looked into my bunk to see Tina lying there with me. She must have felt warm during the night, as she had rolled back a portion of the covers. Hap could now see a part of her uncovered body. Tina had not awakened. Hap looked at me and mouthed silently, "Oh my God," his eyes wide open as if witnessing the most impressive or terrifying thing he had ever seen. Realizing he was staring, I grabbed the blankets and covered her immediately. I gave him a silent head shake, indicating he should leave. He grabbed some clothes from the top of the dresser and left. I put my head back down and fell asleep again. I have no idea how long we lay there, but I was awakened again by Wes coming into the bedroom and calling my name. "What's going on," I said. "Your mom and dad are at the front door and want to come in to visit," he said. "What time is it," I said. "Eleven thirty," he replied. "Holy shit," I said, "Tell them to wait, and I will be out in a minute." "They are in the hallway," Wes said.

"Okay, I just got to get dressed," I said. By then, Tina had awoken and was looking at me for direction. I wasn't sure how to handle this one. Part of me wanted Tina to stay in this room until I could get rid of my parents. Another part of me felt that asking her to do that would be quite cruel. It seemed as though I was embarrassed by her or something. I resolved that we should go. I said, "Get dressed quick."

She put her form-fitting sweat suit back on and ran her fingers through her hair as if to comb it. I quickly put on a pair of jeans and a T-shirt, and we headed to the living room. I told Tina to sit on the loveseat while I went to the door to let my parents in from the hallway. I opened the door and said, "Hi, what are you guys doing today." I gestured for them to come in. "Well, your dad wanted to go to Menards, so we thought we would stop by and see what you were up to," my mother said.

As they entered the living room, they saw Tina sitting on the loveseat. "Hi," Tina said, with a big, sweet smile on her face. My mother had a questioning look on her face. "This is my friend, Tina," I said in an introductory tone. "Tina, this is my mom and dad," I told her, completing the introductions.

"Sit down," I said to my parents, pointing to the couch. They did, and we visited for the next ½ hour. Tina explained that she was in nursing and grew up in Wisconsin Rapids. My dad gave his usual biography about growing up on the farm and joining the Air Force. It included all his stale jokes and his favorite jab at me about not being weened until I was six.

My mother mentioned that she was a nurse also and tried to ask a few questions without much success, as my dad always brought the conversation back to him. Tina listened intently while I sat quietly, hoping that they would have to leave soon. There was a knock at the door to make things even more interesting. I opened it to see Becky standing there with a couple of books in her hand. "Hi," I said, "What's Up?" She said, " I'm just bringing back those two books I borrowed from you." She then acted as if she wanted to come into the apartment. I took the books from her and stood before her so she couldn't go in or see into the apartment. "My mom and dad are here to talk to me," I said, "Can I call you later?" She looked at me kind of funny because I think she wanted to come in and say hi to them. "Yes, that will be alright," she said with a questioning look. "It would be better," I said, "I think something is going on with my sister Janet, and they want to talk privately about it," I said to answer her look. "Oh," she said, "Ya, just give me a call later, and we can talk." "Thanks," I said, and she turned around and headed down the stairs. I closed the door and brought the books back inside. My mother must have heard some of the conversation as she gave me a slightly dirty look. My dad was oblivious to anything and just kept talking to Tina. Then, for no good reason except to throw me from the frying pan and into the fire, my mother said, " We thought we would take you out for supper tonight; maybe Tina would like to go with us." I thought Tina would jump off the couch and kiss me or my mother. "I guess so," I said, "What time'? My mother explained they would go to Menards, visit my sister at UW-L if she was there, and be back to pick us up around 4:00. Then they left and headed on their errands. Tina said, "I better go get cleaned up" "See you at 4:00," she cheered as she gave me a quick kiss and bounded out of the apartment and down the stairs. Oh, shit, I thought to myself as I went back into my room, made up my bunk, and then got into the shower. I knew I was in deep, and there wouldn't be a happy ending for someone, more than likely me.

Wes and Hap had come back home after being at the grocery store. I told them the whole story, and they tried to be supportive, but I could tell they secretly enjoyed this drama. The time to go came, and Tina showed up in some tight-fitting dress slacks with a beaded white sweater. She looked great and glowed about her. My folks pulled up, and we got into the backseat. We drove to West Salem to eat at the Westview Inn, which was one of my parent's favorite spots.

Tina was glued to me the whole time in the backseat, occasionally giving me a peck on the cheek. Supper went well, and I could see that Tina felt like she was part of the family. We returned home around 9ish, and my folks dropped us at the door. I told Tina that I had some studying to do for the rest of the night because there was a technical run-through of our play on Sunday, and I would be at the Fine Arts Center most of the day. *Another lie.* She accepted it, kissed me goodbye, and headed across the street to Marion Hall. I went back into the apartment to find that everyone else was gone.

I picked up the phone and called Becky. I said I was home now and maybe she could drive over. She agreed, and I sat on the couch and waited. Becky arrived, and I kissed her and apologized for being short in the afternoon. She said, "That's okay; my family has its share of problems that my parents deal with." We sat on the couch and talked while I made up a story about my sister fighting with one of her roommates during a party and then calling my parents about maybe living in another house.

She understood, and that ended that subject. We were getting cozy together on the couch and reacquainted with each other, having not had any private time for the whole week. After a few minutes, there was a knock at the door. I opened it to find Tina standing in the hallway with a big smile. I quickly stepped into the hallway, closing the door behind me. "Can I come in?" she asked. "No," I said. "Why not?" she insisted. "I've got company in there," I said in a rather regretful and shameful tone. She looked at me like I had just run over her puppy. Her eyes immediately filled with tears, and she turned away, sobbing, and then ran down the stairs. I knew how she was feeling, and for once, I was the one who was responsible. I thought about a foot tall and tried swallowing the lump in my throat.

I returned to the apartment, and Becky asked, "Who was that so late at night." I lied again and said, "It was this girl that Hap was trying to break up with, and she was looking for him. She was pretty upset when I told her he wasn't here."

"Oh, Becky said. I thought I heard crying." We finished our visit, and I walked her downstairs to her car on the street. We kissed good night, and she went home. I went back upstairs and laid on my bunk. I could not sleep thinking about Tina's face and what a dick I had been to her. If someone had told me I could do that to another person, I would have bet my life against it. I had become the type of person I had always despised.

A person who didn't take other peoples' feelings into account. A liar. A cheat. I never dared to tell Becky what had happened. I tried to talk to Tina again to apologize and ask for forgiveness.

She looked at me with disdain whenever I approached and would walk away. I would never get the chance to apologize. It taught me a lesson. I was thankful that Becky and I were still together, and I would never jeopardize my relationship with her again for the sake of my ego or bragging rights among my peers. I was learning as much outside the College classroom as in. The courses to come would continue to get more complex.

Chapter Eight:

Turnabout Is Fair Play

We finished in second place at the American College Theater Festival. A school out of Wheaton, Illinois, took first place with their production of "Equus." They earned it. The performance was outstanding, and the lead actor got the best actor award at the festival. Our review was positive, and I was happy with my feedback. Our main issues were with the staging of the play and some decisions made by the director.

I would stay busy again for the second semester until the end of the school year. I played the part of Kulighin in "The Three Sisters," a Chekov play. Then, I was cast by a senior for his senior project as "Jean" in "Miss Julie" by August Strindberg.

In that play, I worked with Linda Balgord as Miss Julie. Linda was a freshman student from New Lisbon, Wisconsin. Linda was a quiet, intelligent, pleasant girl of moderate looks. She had thin, wispy brown hair and very defined facial features. Her eyes were big and round with long cow-like eyelashes, her nose was straight and pointed, her cheekbones were high and easily accented, and her mouth was large. It almost appeared as though she had more teeth than most people.

They, of course, were nearly perfect. She didn't care much for foolishness or sophomoric flirtations from the campus "Casanovas." She made it clear that she had a boyfriend back home that she was true to. I admired her for that. What everyone admired Linda for was her singing voice.

It put everyone in the Theater Department to shame. It put most of the music majors to shame as well. She had been blessed with an instrument like Shirley Jones or Barbara Streisand and knew how to use it. Linda would be cast in many musicals and steal the show. She eventually graduated from Viterbo and found professional success in Chicago. Later, she would move to Broadway to star in the ongoing production of "Cats."

She appeared on television performing "Memories" from that show. Later, no less than Andrew Lloyd Weber sought her out and wrote a play, especially for her, called "Sunset Boulevard." Linda was nominated for a number of awards and continues in professional theater to this day.

I also continued to work in the scene shop and made another new acquaintance in the theater department. It was Jay Scott, the younger brother of one of the senior students, Paul Scott. Jay had transferred to Viterbo as a sophomore from St. Johns in Minnesota. He had gone there hoping to play football, but it didn't work out. Jay was working in the scene shop for work-study as well. Jay was about my height and weight. He had an athlete-toned muscular body, curly light brown hair, a round nose, and thick lips, and he wore some of the most viscous square-lensed style wire-rimmed glasses I had ever seen.

Like his older brother, he had terrible eyesight and seemed nearly blind without his glasses. Jay was like many jocks that I had known. He was loud, opinionated, and physically expressive.

By that, I mean he would often poke, punch, or grab people when talking or making a point. He often put people in a headlock as a joke, which wasn't always well received. He had no idea that he might hurt someone and laughed when doing something to someone, thinking they would understand he was kidding them. That's how jocks communicate with each other. He would often challenge me to a shoving match or arm-punching contest to see who was "dominant," for lack of a better term. I never backed down and gave him as good as he gave. He liked that for some reason. He was not a stupid person. I believe he had a reasonably high level of intelligence when he decided to activate his brain instead of his brain. We became friends and enjoyed playing one-on-one basketball, tennis, and other sports together.

We also had a good time at Wunderbar, often taking advantage of the three-for-a-dollar "Shorty Budwieser" deal. He was also politically aware and, at that time, an active left-leaning Jimmie Carter liberal. I was on the other side of the fence so that we would engage in some spirited debates. Eventually, we decided to consider being roommates for our junior year. I knew Wes and Jeff were graduating, and Hap had decided that he would continue living on campus and concentrate on getting a major in business as well.

As time passed, I would refer to Jay by the nickname I had given him, "Scotty." It gave us a kind of Captain Kirk and Mr. Scott kind of Star Trek relationship. It also made it easier for others when referring to "Jay" in the Theater Department.

Becky and I continued our relationship without any issues. We were both busy with our studies and enjoyed having each other to share our lives. We studied together, discussed our roles within the department productions, and became closer with each passing day. As the year was coming to a close, Becky asked if we could have a serious discussion about the upcoming school year.

I agreed, and we found a quiet corner of the fine arts center away from all distractions. Becky told me that she had enough credits with the upcoming summer school to be able to graduate early by the end of the first semester next year. She had been talking with her parents, and she was planning on moving to New York to attend the Lee Strasburg School for acting to pursue her career further there. She wanted to know how I felt about that, and if I would consider going with her, so we wouldn't be apart.

I didn't know what to say; I was at a loss for words. I told her how much I loved her and wanted the best for her. I was proud of her accomplishment and understood why she wanted to go. I reminded her that I needed to graduate and I certainly didn't have the money to go to New York. She told me she loved me too and wasn't sure if she could leave me. She said she thought her parents would be willing to help with the financial situation that New York would present. I told her she should go and I would be back here waiting. If our relationship was true, we should be able to make it work.

We were both scared at the idea but decided to concentrate on living from one day to the next until it was time for her to leave. We held each other close for a few minutes and then returned to the rest of the world.

The school year was winding down, and I felt terrific about where I was in the theater department. I was probably the most technically skilled student in set construction, lighting, sound, and all the other stage crafts.

I understood my acting abilities and felt like I could handle any role. I was becoming more interested in directing and was looking forward to some of the classes over the next year that would allow me to try it out. Scotty and I solidified our plan to live together in the fall, and he would be looking for an off-campus rental for him and me during the summer. I was headed back home to work construction for the summer. Becky was doing summer theater again, and before we said our goodbyes, she clarified that she didn't like the idea of me living with Scotty in the fall. She didn't like him very much. She thought he was rude, overbearing, and obnoxious. She also felt like she needed to caution me about his use of marijuana.

She was right. Scotty had an affinity for smoking pot. I assured her that was his problem and not mine. I didn't sit around and smoke dope with him. I also reminded her that there were not that many guys in the department that I could room with. She restated her objections about me living with Scotty and wouldn't let me forget her warnings should some trouble arise. I changed the subject and confirmed with her that I would see her shows this summer and also to Chatfield for Western Days again. "You better," she said. We took a minute to look into each other's eyes and then kissed goodbye.

The summer flew by, and I could get to the summer theater productions and touch base with Becky after the shows. Working for Strongs was hot and harrowing again, and I had decided on the last day that I would need to pick something different in the future for my summer income. The sun just fried me, and I couldn't enjoy anything outside, away from work. That night, I asked my friend Ted Wise if he wanted to go to Chatfield with me the next day to see the Western Days Production and the huge house that Becky lived in. The last night of the summer at work was always a celebration for those leaving. We went to the Airport Bar and shortly started after the day ended. We ate early and then drank the night away.

For some reason, I felt compelled to indulge beyond what I had in the past. Shortly after midnight, I decided I better head for home. My folks were on vacation, so I had the house to myself. I staggered in and realized in short order that I was going to have a long night. The bed spins led to multiple puke sessions in the bathroom, and I also suffered the crushing headache of alcohol poisoning. I couldn't sleep in my bed, so I stayed on the bathroom floor. By about 4 am, I was still suffering horribly and decided to sleep in the bathtub with the shower running to give my body some other sensation and maybe allow it to relax. It worked until the water started to get cold. I put the plugin and let the tub fill.

I slept there until I heard my alarm in the bedroom at 7:00. Ted was coming around 8:00, and we would drive to Chatfield. I grabbed a bottle of pop and gagged down a couple of Tylenol and some Rolaids, hoping to relieve the headache and nausea. Ted showed up, and I climbed in. We headed out listening to the 8-track of the Beach Boys while I told him of my self-induced malaise. I rolled the window down and hung my head in the opening, hoping to force some fresh air into my body.

We talked about the usual stuff along the way, and I actually started to recover slowly. By the time we reached Chatfield, I felt nearly human again. I directed Ted to Becky's house, and we pulled up on the street outside so as not to block the driveway. Ted was excited to tour the mansion as I had described in great detail how big and fancy I thought it was. From the outside, he confirmed what I had previously said. I rang the doorbell and waited for Becky to answer.

She came to the door, and we hugged, kissed each other quickly, and invited Ted and me inside. There was some small talk, and I told her about my foolish night of drinking. She gave Ted and me the tour of the house, and we talked about where we might go and have something to eat. The phone rang, and Becky went into the kitchen to answer it. Ted and I stayed in the family room. After a few minutes, Becky entered and said she needed to talk to me. We went back into the kitchen. Becky then told me that the phone call was for her. It was one of the actors she had worked with during the summer theater, and he was calling to say he had come to Chatfield from Madison on the Greyhound Bus to see her.

He was waiting at the bus stop downtown for her to come and get him. "Why would he be coming here to see you," I asked. She then explained that they had become good friends during summer theater, and she mentioned "Western Days." She didn't think he would come to see her, but he did. I was stunned. I could tell by the look on her face that she wasn't being candid with me. Maybe that was the same look I had on my face during the Tina Cain fiasco. I told her there was no way I could stay here with him being here as well.

Not to mention how embarrassing it was to have Ted there to witness this debacle. I told her I was leaving and never to talk to me again. I didn't scream or get mad or cry or anything. I was void of emotion at that point. I told Ted that we needed to leave and we would talk about it in the car on the way home.

So, Ted and I left. On the way, I told him what had happened and apologized that he had wasted his day driving over there. Most of the time, I just sat silently, looking at the white line outside my window and listening to the music on the 8-track. I will return to LaCrosse on Monday to meet with Scotty and move into our apartment. My enthusiasm for theater, school, and life, in general, was nearly all gone. I went deep inside myself, trying to find the desire to continue. I owed it to my parents to finish what I started, but I could have cared less. I would later refer to this period in my life as my "Blue Period." If I were a truly great artist, my best creations would result from this prolonged desperation. In reality, I just felt like shit.

Chapter Nine:

Now What

O n Monday, I went to LaCrosse and met Scotty at the apartment he picked for us on Johnson Street, about four blocks south of Viterbo and the Fine Arts Center. It was not what I had expected. The rent was cheap at $135.00 per month, so I have no idea why I thought this would be a nice place. As I looked at it, I could only think of some "crack house" you might see in a low-budget cop movie. It was a two-story duplex with failing forest green shingle siding, four windows, two up and two down, that had no storms and the glass in nearly all of them was cracked. The roof had an excellent sag in the middle, like an old horse you might ride at a dude ranch. A stairwell on the outside right of the building went up to the second-floor unit; that was ours, naturally. The stairwell was originally not covered, but at some point in history, a group of drunks must have gotten tired of shoveling the snow off them, so they constructed a covering. It was just tall enough for someone less than 6 feet tall to stand in. The stairs were worn in the middle, so their thickness was about ½ of what they were on each end. The hallway going up was steep and dark, with a nice bare light bulb at the top. It gave a good view of the number of bats that had sought shelter. An old wooden entry door at the top took you into the kitchen. On the right were two lower and two upper cabinets with the only countertop in between. Someone must have painted it white at least 20 times. The floor was a turn-of-the-century linoleum of red flowers and black-lined white squares. The lack of shine was evident, as the wear had exposed a significant amount of the underlying black layer. It had a lovely quarter-inch pitch toward the sink that hung on the wall to the left. There was only the sink and no cabinet underneath. The sink reminded me of a shop sink you might see in an old gas station garage. On the far wall was a small apartment-size gas stove next to a large gas space heater, which was the sole source of heat for the unit. There was a newer frig on the right next to the cabinets. The walls were lathe and plaster except for one paneled wall in each bedroom. How modern! Scotty was so proud of his find and showed me what *really* sold him on the place.

Off the kitchen was a door to the roof of a covered porch down below. Here, we could put this Hibachi grill and a couple of chairs. Wow, our own veranda with a view of the backyard neighbors. We could sit and drink beers on nice days as long as we didn't stand in the same spot to be safe from falling onto the porch below. He was also nice enough to give me the smaller of the two bedrooms, featuring no closet and a nice 12-inch x 12-inch square cut-out of the entry door at the perfect height so it wouldn't hit the corner of the single bed behind it. The only decent room was the living room, big enough for a sofa and a couple of chairs. It also had carpet on the floor, the thickness of an inexpensive bath towel. Somehow, it seemed like the right place for me and my attitude for life then.

Scotty was excited about the year ahead. He told me that his grandfather had passed away over the summer and left him a healthy sum of money. He had purchased a 77 silver and black Monte Carlo with a black "Landau Roof" and a top-level stereo system. He also purchased a Martin 12-string guitar, which he had no idea how to play but was going to teach himself. He bought a beautiful stereo system with all the bells and whistles I appreciated, and he still had plenty left over to purchase a 6-month weed supply. He put the phone and utilities in his name, and I agreed to pay half. We went to the grocery store and got all the essentials—a loaf of bread, a dozen eggs, some hot dogs and buns, a twelve-pack of Mountain Dew, and a case of beer. We were set.

We both started working immediately in the scene shop to prepare for the fall semester's first big production. I had avoided going into the green room to avoid seeing Becky; she and I didn't talk in any of the classes we shared. A number of the students expressed their sadness that we were no longer the couple who, in their words, "were made for each other." Father Recker and Sister Marie Leon said nothing about the subject, and I felt like Father was glad. Outside the department, I spent most of my time at Wunderbar or home on our veranda. One afternoon, Becky called our apartment. Scotty must have given her the number. She wanted to talk about what had happened. She insisted that she hadn't done anything wrong, meaning she hadn't slept with that guy and had no continued contact with him. I couldn't bring myself to be anything other than hurt and angry. I asked her how we could stay together once she was in New York when we struggled over the summer here. I needed time to think.

The year's first production was the musical "Fiddler on the Roof." I had done it in high school and was looking forward to having a chance to play the lead "Tevye." As it turned out, Father Recker announced that the part of Tevye was going to be played by a guest artist from the Broadway Production. His name was Paul Lipson. He took over for Zero Mostel on Broadway and holds the record for playing Tevye more than anyone else in history. It was exciting to think we could participate with a professional actor. It also meant that my only role would probably be Lazar Wolfe, the butcher. That's what I got. I also was one of the bottle dancers. I had done the bottle dance in the high school production but found out it wasn't quite as easy, being 30 pounds heavier and almost 6" taller. Becky would land the part of Yente the Matchmaker. The rest of the casting went as I expected. I was in tune with what Father sought in actors and how he viewed our department members. At the auditions, there were also many first-year students from theater majors. I remember watching them and thinking I hoped I didn't look that bad at my first audition. One of the girls did alright. Her name was Jessie Birk. She was from the small town of Millville, Minnesota, nestled along the Zumbro River about 25 miles northeast of Rochester. At Wunderbar, after the auditions, she walked in with the other freshman, and as they came by our table, I told her I thought she would get the part of the youngest daughter, "Chava." She looked at me so surprised and wondered how I could know that. I told her just to wait and see the cast list outside the greenroom tomorrow. Sure enough, she got the part. A couple of nights later, we were sitting at Wunderbar at our usual corner table, and Jessie and the other freshman girls came in again. Scotty and I invited them to our table to talk and bought them a few beers. I thought Jessie was attractive and had a small-town innocence about her. She hung up on every word I said about theater and couldn't believe how good my audition was and how I knew who would get each part. I ate up the attention and played the deep-thinking intellectual theater artist advising on how to make it at Viterbo. Eventually, I decided that I might like to get to know her in a more male/female sort of way. Feeling lucky, I invited her to visit my "bachelor pad" and watch a movie. I have to admit I had every intention of taking advantage of her. I had decided that from now on, I would be in control of what happened and when in my relationships with women. Jessie was going to be my first adventure. She arrived; I got us a couple of beers, and we sat on the couch to watch the movie. She told me about herself and her family. She is the oldest of nine children—seven girls and two boys—and grew up on a farm. She went to Elgin-Millville High School and wore her high school letter jacket. As the night progressed, I was less interested in the movie and more interested in what was underneath that letter jacket. We started kissing, and I made my move. She guarded herself and told me she wasn't ready for that yet. I accepted that. We watched the rest of the movie, and I walked her back to the dorm. We agreed that we could see each other again. I was happy with that, and having someone other than Becky on my mind was nice. Over the next few weeks, Jessie and I would spend more and more time together and eventually develop a relationship. She gave and supported me and did many things like making me dinners, cleaning our apartment, and scrubbing my back in the bathtub. We would also have an intense physical relationship unlike any I had. It helped me heal and motivated me to continue pursuing my theater education. We didn't talk much about our feelings for each other. We talked about Fiddler rehearsals and school classes. She wasn't enjoying living in the dorm and was being harassed by some of the other girls on 3rd South. Of course, 3rd South was the legendary home of the gossip girls and maybe, unfortunately for Jessie, Tina Cain. It didn't take long for her to start staying at my apartment. While walking back to the Fine Arts Center from Murphy Center one afternoon, I heard someone call my name from behind. I stopped and turned around to see who. It was Becky. She stopped in the middle of the street as I turned. "Can I talk to you for a minute?" she asked. I said sure and approached to avoid having to shout. When I got close, she wanted to know how I was doing. I told her that I was fine but had been very busy. She then wanted to tell me that she had heard some talk about me and Jessie that she didn't think was very flattering. It especially bothered her to think that I was letting her wash my back in the tub and that she might stay overnight. I was surprised at how guilty I felt having her almost scold me like my mother might. I waited for her to finish, secretly hoping she would ask me to stop seeing Jessie and that she wanted us to get back together. She didn't. Trying not to get angry or be a smart ass, I told her that what I do really isn't anyone else's business. My relationship with Jessie isn't hurting anyone, so I would appreciate it if people left me and her alone. We stood there silent for a moment, just looking at each other, and I almost leaned in to hug and kiss her like I used to. I just told her I needed to get to the scene shop and left her standing in the street. It bothered me for the rest of the day. Deep down, I knew I still had real feelings for her that I thought I needed to squash. I wasn't going to hurt Jessie like I did Tina.

It was Fiddler's final week of rehearsal, and Paul Lipson showed up from New York to take over for the stand-in who had worked with the cast for the first five weeks. Paul was in costume each night and often stopped Father to insert what he would call some business into the scene. That meant he had some "schtick," as the Jewish comics would call it that was not written in the script but would get a big laugh in certain places. It worked, and we were all impressed by his energy, awareness, and effortless creation of his character. It made a difference to the entire cast. He was like a great athlete who could elevate the play of others on the team. He didn't lecture us, give classes, or comment on anyone's acting. He only suggested things based on his 2000-plus performances of the show and what he had seen that worked. We listened intently and did our best to follow his advice.

On opening night, we were all backstage and very excited as the show had been a sellout. 1200 seats would be filled for the first time in our experience. Paul sat quietly on a folding chair, waiting for the curtain to rise. I asked him how he could remain so calm before a performance. He told me that Zero Mostel had given him some advice and he would share it with me. He said, "Zero Mostel told me to remember, the audience is not coming to see you." It wasn't meant as a slight. It was the truth and an excellent tip for any actor. The audience comes to see the character you portray, so forget about yourself on stage. I never forgot that advice, and in my life, I found it applies to many situations. We are never quite as important as we think. Every person we meet sees us through their eyes and not ours. So be careful what character you portray.

We had three performances of the show—Friday night, Saturday night, and a Sunday Matinee. After the matinee, we would all go to Friar Tucks Tavern and Restaurant across Jackson Street behind the Fine Arts Center for the cast party. Jessie and I arrived and found a place to sit near the back of the banquet room. Everyone was in a great mood because this was the first (and, as it turned out, only) time the college would foot the bill for a cast party. Usually, the cast party was for those who wanted to hit Wunderbar.

Never any food and pay for your drinks. Becky came into the room and walked directly up to our table. She looked at me and said, "I need to talk to you when this ends. Would you mind coming over afterward?"

I looked at Jessie, and she looked back at me, wondering what this could be about. I asked Jessie, "Do you mind if I talk to her after?" Jessie said that she didn't. "Ok, I told Becky." "When we finish here, I will stop over." The party continued for a few hours, and everyone had a great time. When it finished, I told Jessie to go to the apartment and wait for me until I was done with Becky.

I didn't think it would take very long. I just figured she was going to give me one more lecture about the life I was living. When I arrived, she was the only one home that was unusual. She invited me in, and we sat across from each other at the kitchen table. She started to talk, and tears came to her eyes. She wanted me to know how much she loved me and cared for me and if there was any way we could make things work out. I looked deep into her eyes as she spoke. This was real. I swallowed hard and tried to keep my composure. I told her I loved her too, but many things happened between us. I wanted her to be able to go to New York and make it big without having to worry about me. She reminded me that I could come with her and make it together. I sat quietly without responding, and we just looked at each other. In my mind, I was thinking about everything Jessie and I had done together over the last few weeks, how Jessie gave herself to me for the first time. How caring she seemed and willing to put me first. Was that love, and did I love her? I couldn't answer. As much as I wanted to agree to putting Becky and me back together, I just couldn't do it. Becky knew me better than anyone. I had never loved anyone more than her.

Eventually, I apologized to her, saying it might be most suitable for us to part ways. I finally told her I was sorry and it would be best just to say goodbye. I told her I hoped the best for her New York adventure and that I would be thinking of her. She began openly crying, and again, I fought the urge to hug her and give her one more kiss goodbye. "I have to go now," I said. I left her crying in the kitchen. As I got outside the building, it was dark, and I was looking for someplace to collapse. My eyes were filled with tears, and I had trouble breathing. I kept stumbling along the sidewalk toward home. I remember saying out loud, "Oh God, what should I do?" I felt like somebody just died. When I arrived home, Hap and Wes happened to be there visiting Scotty and taking in some of his stash. They stared at me and asked, "What happened to you?" I fought through sobs to tell them of my break-up with Becky. How bad I felt about leaving her crying. I was inconsolable.

I asked where Jessie was, and Scotty told me she left thinking I wasn't returning. It made me even more upset. I got on the phone and called her right away. I told her I needed you and could you please come over immediately. She agreed, and I went into my room. When Jessie arrived, I heard Wes tell her that I was in my room and that he had never seen me like that. She came in, and I asked her just to hold me. She lay with me on the bed, and I cried myself to sleep in her arms. Losing Becky would be something I couldn't forget for the rest of my life. I had become a ship without a rudder, and my life decisions going forward wandered from one wreck to another.

Chapter Ten:

Millville Madness

Before long, the semester was ending, and the break for Christmas was right around the corner. Becky was gone, off to New York and her chance to star on the "Great White Way." Jessie and I were working hard at school and in the scene shop. We were becoming closer and closer all the time. She was always there for me, and the drama surrounding Becky and my relationship wasn't part of Jessie and me. We decided to go to her house for one weekend during the break so I could meet her family. Neither of us had a vehicle, so she called home, and her brother Jeff and sister Jenny would pick us up and drive us to Millville. Around 5:00 pm on a dark Friday night, a little white Pontiac Sunbird pulled up in front of Marion Hall with the radio blaring and two high school kids smoking in the front seat. It was Jessie's brother and sister to get us. They both got out of the car with big smiles on their faces. Jeff was a tall, thin, muscular farm kid with a rough complexion and a voice strained by what sounded like nodes on his vocal cords. The sound of his voice always made you want to clear your own throat. Jenny was a blonde, blue-eyed, slightly smaller version of Jessie. We all met, and then Jeff grabbed our bags and put them into the trunk. Jessie and I crawled into the backseat with no room between us, and my knees pressed against the back of the front seat. Jessie ordered them to turn down the radio and scolded them for smoking in the car. She clarified that there would be no smoking on the way home. They didn't argue; it was just a small preview of what I would learn later. Jessie was the oldest and rode herd on all her siblings. She had no problem bossing them around the house, giving them chores, and mothering them. The ride took us up Highway 61 past Winona toward Wabasha. Just a few miles short of Wabasha, we turned off 61 to the west at a little spot called Weaver. It had a little store and a few houses tucked on the hillside at the bottom of the bluffs. We headed upward and climbed the bluff on a little paved road that must have been a logging trail. The hill was a good 2 miles long, and I wondered if it would ever end. Our ears started popping just as we crested the top. From there, the road winded back and forth through the farm fields on both sides. It was so dark except for the occasional yard light as we passed the farmhouse. Eventually, we came to a hard right turn, and the road widened and became perfectly straight for the next 6 miles. In the distance, you could see the glow of the town of Plainview and the light on top of the water tower. Finally, I thought there was civilization in this wilderness. We turned right at the only stop light and went west through town and back out into the darkness of the countryside. About 5 miles out of town, we turned north on Cty. Rd. 2 and headed for Millville. The road twisted and turned up and down until, eventually, heading down a long hill toward the river bottom. Before getting to the bottom, we turned north again on a dirt town road that climbed a small hill and headed into the country again. After about a mile, we turned back west onto what I would learn was the driveway to the house. It was about the width of 1 ½ cars and looked more like a field road than a drive. It had some gravel and was badly rutted in spots. Into the blackness, we traveled for another mile before the road dropped down again, and the glow of the light broke the darkness. We turned 90 degrees into the yard past an old barn. The driveway more or less just ended and opened up into what looked like a river delta. There was a mix of mud and grass and gravel. They parked facing the hill that was north of the house. A scruffy mutt of a dog started barking and limped his way toward the car as we got out. I could hear the rusty squeak of the windmill on the hill as it spun around, filling the cistern with water that gravity-fed the house. There was a granary on the hill as well. Jeff and Jenny yelled at the dog to shut up as we approached the house. In my mind, I had seen this house before. It was in every PBS documentary on the poverty of Appalachia. It was a big white square house with white aluminum siding and a metal roof. We stepped onto a patio covered with a green indoor/outdoor carpet. There was a homemade picnic table sitting there and a broken-down charcoal grill. The only light was coming through the glass of the patio doors in the middle of the east wall. This is the entry used as the front entry on the south side of the house. It was at the top of a set of precast concrete steps that had pulled so far away from the house that it was a bit of a challenge to step off them into the doorway. As we got closer, I could see the patio door glass was riddled with dirty hand prints and all kinds of nose and slobber marks from the dog looking in. Directly in front of the door were two old aluminum cook pots holding dog food in one and water in the other. We stepped over and entered into a large kitchen. The kitchen floor had what looked like new brown and black patterned linoleum. The walls were paneling. There were solid, dark, stained oak kitchen cabinets to the right. There was a brown older model gas stove and a yellow refrigerator. A large, more modern wood stove was in the middle of the kitchen, back against the wall. It was in use as you could feel the heat immediately upon entering the room and smell the wood burning. Jeff and Jenny disappeared around the corner and up the stairwell. Jessie and I stood in the kitchen so she could introduce her parents. Standing in front of the stove cooking was Jessie's mother, Mary. She was a slightly framed woman of 39, with blonde hair, blue eyes, and a pleasing smile. "Hi," she said. "I'm Mary. Very nice to meet you, Jay." She stuck out her hand to shake. I was amazed at how young and small she looked, considering she had given birth to nine children. "Nice to meet you as well," I said, shaking her hand. Then I heard a loud, raspy voice say, "What took you so long." Sitting at the table in the kitchen was Jessie's father. He was a short, well-built man with a shiny bald head with blonde hair slicked back on both sides. He had a large nose on which was a large red boil. He was smoking a cigarette and drinking a brandy seven. He spoke loudly like someone who was hard of hearing or always worked around loud machinery. Jessie answered, "We came as fast as we could, Dad." He then introduced himself. "I'm Jessie's dad, Jack Birk. You want a drink before supper?"

"No, sir, I'm good," I said. Jessie and I sat down at the kitchen table. It was an oval-shaped gray Formica table top with a hodge-podge of mismatched chairs around it in various stages of disrepair. I noticed a large saw cut through a good portion of one end of the table where someone must have attempted to cut a board with a circle saw and cut the table along with it. Shortly, there was the noise of a herd of children coming down the stairs. It rumbled and shook the house as if we had a bowling alley above us. The kids were excited to see who their big sister had brought home. It wasn't anything like meeting the Von Trapp children of the Sound of Music. They flowed into the kitchen bright-eyed and bushy-tailed as Jessie introduced them in order. Jeff, Jenny, Julie, Jordie, Jackie, Jill, Jane and Justin. It was a study in genetics. Most had blonde hair, blue eyes, and freckles that easily made them recognizable to outsiders that they would be siblings. The unique two of the bunch were Jeff, the oldest boy with dark curly hair, and Jordie, one of the middle daughters with dark, flowing, almost brunette hair. She was striking in appearance with a natural beauty that made me think she could have been Jacquelyn Smith's child. Jill and Jane were identical twins. They were challenging to tell apart and even shared the same chipped front tooth that I was told occurred when they ran into each other. That is one of those things you ask: "What are the chances?" I wouldn't have believed it if I hadn't seen it with my own eyes. They all looked at me excitedly and took turns asking me questions. I gave them answers, a few jokes, and silly remarks for the smaller kids to make them laugh. I couldn't help but feel like these kids were starving for someone from the outside world to engage with. They lived on such a long, dead-end road in the middle of nowhere that it wasn't like their friends would ride bikes to see them. Mary told the kids to wash up for supper while Jessie helped her set the table and put the food on. I noticed that most plates and place settings didn't match, and everybody had their favorite glass to drink. The meal was a delicious baked ham with mashed potatoes and surprisingly fresh sweet corn from the neighbor who rented and tilled the land around them. They also farmed a portion of the 20 acres that Jessie's family owned, providing some income yearly. After dinner, we sat at the kitchen table and played 500 with her parents. Jessie's dad took out a bottle of Mr. Boston Five Star Brandy, insisting that we all must have a drink. He ensured we knew it was the best brandy we would ever taste. We had more than one drink over the next few hours as we played game after game. Jessie's dad was drinking more than the rest of us and would talk louder and louder with each new pour. Around 10:30, he was obviously drunk and becoming less friendly with everyone. Mary decided it was time to quit, so everyone but Jack indicated they were ready for bed. Jessie took me upstairs to the room I would be sleeping in. The stairway was narrow, with minimal steps at a fairly steep angle. At the top of the stairs, there were four bedrooms. She took me to the one straight ahead. She opened the door to reveal a small bedroom not much bigger than a closet with a bunk bed on the right and a small dresser on the left. There was just enough room for someone to walk in between. I noticed a window on the far wall covered by plastic billowing in and out with the wind. This was her brother's room, which they shared normally, but it was the guest room for tonight. The brothers would sleep downstairs on the couch in the living room. She hugged and kissed me good night and told me to call if I needed any more blankets. I got undressed and crawled under the 3 or 4 comforters on the bottom bunk. The mattress slouched underneath me, something like a hammock. The beddings appeared delicate, covered in tiny fabric balls, creating the sensation of reclining on a beach of grains. I closed my eyes and tried my best to fall asleep. The noise of the plastic on the window grew as the wind out of the north made the room colder as the night went on. There was no heat in the upstairs except from the stairway. As soon as I nod off, someone would get up from their bed and head downstairs to the bathroom, making enough noise to wake me again. With seven girls, this went on about every hour throughout the night. At one point, my door opened, and Jessie came in, closing it behind her. She crawled under the covers with me and asked if I was staying warm. I asked her what she was doing. Her father was only sleeping one room away, and I could hear him wheezing for every breath for most of the night. I was sure he would wake up anytime, and if he found his daughter in bed with me, decide to shoot me. Jessie laughed and said he was passed out like always and couldn't hear anything. We snuggled until it was just too uncomfortable in that little bed. She got up and returned to her room, and I tried to get to sleep finally. I couldn't help but feel sorry for these kids living like this, but I was impressed by how it didn't bother them. I thought I saw my breath, so I covered my head and fell asleep. What had I gotten myself into?

Chapter Eleven:

The Show Must Go On

The second semester started with auditions for our next main stage production, "The Diary of Anne Frank." I landed the part of Mr. Frank, who was the show's male lead. Mary Hare would get the part of Anne Frank. It was kind of unusual to see a pair of red-haired people land the roles of Jewish characters, but it worked because Mary certainly looked like she could have been my daughter. As miscast as we might have been appearance-wise, I have to say we both may have had our best performances. We received standing ovations each night, which hadn't happened before. Looking back, it might have just been an ovation for the characters and the story. How could anyone not see the story and be moved by the courage of Anne, Mr. Frank, and the others?

Jessie was struggling with school and said she considered not continuing next year. She just didn't like the college atmosphere and found the rest of her courses more work outside of theater classes than she wanted. I offered to help her in any way, but it was a decision she and her parents should make. I was getting very busy with upper-class coursework and serving as the head student in the scene shop. For the last production of the year, a guest director was brought in to do "Romeo and Juliet" in the shadow box theater. Having so much experience in the technical area, I was assigned as the assistant lighting designer and responsible for running the light board for the show. It had over 100 light cues, which is nearly one every other minute. I wanted to audition for the part of Romeo, but Father let me know that he intended for Scotty to get that part as he needed some experience. He certainly looked the part, but his verbal skills were lacking. Shakespeare is poetry and needs someone to "turn a verse" with clarity and meaning. He did his best, and the story is always better than the actors.

Jessie came to me toward the end of the semester and said she was afraid she might be pregnant. The reality of our relationship hit me in the face like an icy-packed snowball. It turned out to be a false alarm, but I felt like it was time to stop playing around and decide if Jessie and I would have a serious future together. A few weeks later, I put $50 down on an engagement ring and asked her to marry me. She was surprised but thrilled and said yes. From that point forward, we started making decisions together. She would quit college and find work somewhere in Lacrosse for the summer. I would continue and get my degree and see if there was work I do in Lacrosse for the summer. We would get our apartment that summer, and if possible, I would work part-time, go to school, and finish. Her siblings were more excited about the news than anyone. Both sets of parents were supportive but skeptical. We planned on getting married the summer after I graduated and seeing what would happen afterward.

Graduation came for this year's seniors, and it was time to say goodbye to some of my friends in that class. Most were great kids and probably not going on any further with their theater pursuits. As the seniors gathered in the Fine Arts Center,, preparing for the ceremony, I saw someone I hadn't expected to see. Becky had returned for the ceremony and milled among the senior theater majors. She looked different in a way I couldn't explain—quiet and sullen for what should be a joyous, fun occasion. We never made eye contact, and I didn't try to talk to her. I learned she was returning to Chatfield a few weeks after the ceremony. Apparently, she had been assaulted by someone in New

York, and the event's trauma sent her back home for recovery. This news made me both very sad and angry. I even felt guilty for not being there to protect her. I would hope that someday I can speak with her again and express my sorrow for what she went through.

By the summer, Jessie and I had moved to a first-floor apartment of an old house on 11th Street next to Cass St. in LaCrosse. She had gotten a job at WIZM Z93 Radio station in LaCrosse in the office, posting commercials. I landed a job with Cremer Jewelers in LaCrosse as they expanded to the new Valley View Mall built just outside Onalaska. It helped that I had worked at Bollom's Jewelry store for a high school summer and that Mrs. Cremer was a big fan of Viterbo Theater. We were also lucky that my parents had decided to buy me a car. It was a '70s model Plymouth Fury. It's a good runner with newer tires and decent condition. Thankfully, Jessie could walk to work most days, and I could drive either downtown to Cremer's or out to the new store in the mall. Our life was going very well, and we became closer daily. In the fall of my senior year, I was cast in the first show as Mr. Sycamore in the comedy *You Can't Take It With You*. Once again, the lead of "Grandpa," aka Martin Vanderhoff (a part made famous in the movie by the legendary Lionel Barrymore), went to a guest artist from Broadway named William Griffis. Mr. Griffis was also well known in Hollywood during the '30s and appeared in many movies. He was nearing the end of his acting career but did many character parts on TV shows such as Remington Steele. In a strange twist of fate and without knowing this would be my last appearance on stage. I would not get cast in another show for the rest of my college career. Instead, I would spend time working on my senior project directing and directing a play for LaCrescent High School. I still worked in the scene shop and did technical work for the department. Then, in the second semester, I was one of the seniors who was picked to audition for ABC Television. The casting director, Mary Lynn Henry, was searching for cast members for the daytime soap opera All My Children. I was tasked with picking her up at the airport and taking her to and from her hotel and the college. My audition went very well; I knew it was my best audition ever. Afterward, Mary Lynn gave some general critiques of the auditions and explained what casting directors look for in daytime soap actors and actresses. It was an eye-opening talk as she told us how important our physical appearance was in the selection process. She said you must be attractive, have good clear skin, bright white straight teeth, and be thin, as the camera adds ten pounds, along with other characteristics that had nothing to do with acting ability. As I drove her back to the hotel, she told me I had the acting ability she was looking for and suggested I go to New York for more experience. She could see me in a soap playing what they call the regular guy versus any of the romantic leads. Red-headed, freckle-faced men and women usually played comedy or sidekicks to the leads. I thanked her for the compliment. She said to look her up if I decided to come to New York, and she would help me. I went home and told Jessie, and we discussed what she said. I kept thinking about what happened to Becky in New York and wasn't sure I could handle living in such a big city. With that in mind, I decided to stay with the idea of directing and becoming a theater department head at some small college like Viterbo.

As the year ended, Father made it clear that it was time to decide where to go from Viterbo. He thought I could be an actor, director, or college professor, whichever I chose. He wanted me to go for acting as he thought that was my natural ability. I preferred directing because it was more exciting and less stressful than performing. He helped by giving me a list of graduate schools I could try to get into to pursue directing and a Master of Fine Arts degree. I looked at Stanford in California, Montclair in New Jersey, and Southern Methodist in Texas. Southern Methodist invited me to an audition in Chicago. I had never been to Chicago and didn't know how to drive downtown to the Palmer House, where the auditions would take place.

Taking my parents advice, I had my older brother Jerry drive me down. We left early in the morning on the day of the audition. I was to be there at 9:00 a.m. Just outside Chicago, we ran into a severe thunderstorm with high winds, heavy rain, and hail, bringing all traffic to a standstill. By the time the storm passed, we had less than 20 minutes to get downtown. We arrived in front of the Palmer House at 8:55, and I rushed inside to find where the auditions were held. I followed the signs in the lobby and went up to the mezzanine level.

Come to find out, there were several schools in addition to Southern Methodist holding the same kind of auditions. I asked a few people to help me find the Southern Methodist group. They sent me down the hall, and there was a hotel room with a sign on the door indicating Southern Methodist. I entered to find two middle-aged men sitting at a table and a small chair across the room from them. One of the men looked very much like Jim Croce.

I introduced myself and apologized for being late. Then I asked if I could use the bathroom before I auditioned, as I had been in the car for the last 6 hours. They said yes, and please hurry as they were on a tight schedule. When I returned without any other information or explanation of the process, they told me to go ahead. I sat in the chair and began my audition. The first part went okay, but I forgot my lines when I had to do my Shakespeare portion. Due to the time constraint, they stopped me and did a small personal interview. They gave me the obligatory "We will let you know when it is over." I left the room and knew I had blown it. Six hours in a car through a storm for 20 minutes of failure. The next issue was finding my brother, who dropped me off and had nowhere to park. I sat in the hotel lobby and waited for him to find me. I had no idea where to go looking in downtown Chicago. After about 15 minutes, he came into the hotel and found me. "Did you make it?" he asked. I told him just barely, and it was a total disaster. We took our time coming home and stopped at a McDonalds for lunch. This would be the highlight of the trip.

Jessie and I were planning our wedding for the spring of 1981. We needed to go to the Cathedral in LaCrosse to meet with the priest and take part in what they called the pre-wedding assessment classes before the church and priest would agree to give a Catholic Wedding Mass. We went for a few weeks and completed the classes and then took the final survey questions the priest asked for so we could meet with him and discuss our future. One afternoon, we went to the Cathedral and met with Father Dwyer. He was the typical Catholic priest in appearance: elderly with black horn-rimmed glasses, snow-white hair, and an unhappy look on his face most of the time.

We entered his office, and he went over our information. He complimented us on our efforts in the classes and knowledge of Catholic practices. Based on the information we provided, he was sure our marriage would be successful, as he put it. Then, toward the end of the interview, he asked why we had listed the same address on our paperwork. He thought it must have been some kind of oversight. We told him there was no mistake that we lived together. In an instant, his attitude changed, and he made it clear that there was no way that we could get married in the Cathedral with full mass. Perhaps he could officiate a private service in the basement of the church. I was less than thrilled with this sudden change of heart and asked for a further explanation. He then told me that I was a Lutheran heathen and couldn't possibly understand the biblical reasons for his decision. I told him he had no basis for calling me a heathen, and I had no particular interest in having him or the Cathedral involved with our marriage. I bit my tongue instead of repeating what I thought of him.

Jessie and I left and never returned. Instead, we would go to the Newman Center on the campus of UW-L and meet with Father Al Thomas about getting married. Father Al was a level-headed, gregarious man with a more 20th century understanding of the world and the Catholic church's mission. He was well aware of Father Dwyer and his attitudes. Father Al agreed to marry us and give us a full mass and blessing. This made Jessie very happy and her parents extremely happy. I had decided to become catholic and raise my children as catholic as well. To me, I didn't see that much difference between Catholics or Lutherans. I always judged a person as an individual and not by their religious denomination. Most folks I knew didn't live a 100% lifestyle for any faiths I had seen. Many got saved every Sunday to sin as they pleased the rest of the week. I had to count myself in that group as well.

I heard back from Southern Methodist University, and I wasn't accepted into their program. I wasn't surprised. However, they recommended me to Trinity University at the Dallas Theater Center in Dallas. Without meeting them or talking with anyone there, I was offered a 2-year Graduate Assistantship toward a Master of Fine Arts Degree in theater. Not knowing exactly what that meant, I asked Father Recker what he thought. He seemed to think it was a great opportunity that I should accept. So, I did. I would have to report to the Dallas Theater Center before the end of August to be enrolled. I just took for granted that going to Dallas and being at the theater would be a snap, and it sounded good to everyone I talked to. It would seem that I had learned nothing about decision-making in the last four years. I was so confident about my abilities that it was comical. What is that old saying, "Pride comes before the fall?"

Chapter Twelve:

The Ovation Ends

On March 14, 1981, Jessie and I were married at the Newman Center in LaCrosse. Ryan, Wes, and Jessie's brother Jeff stood up with me. Jeff Luchsinger played his 12-string guitar and provided the music. The ceremony went like clockwork, and we looked into each other's eyes, making the most important vows of our lives. The reception was fun, and everyone seemed to have a great time. We didn't go on a honeymoon because we had no money.

We borrowed to pay for many of the wedding items ourselves. Jessie's dress alone was almost $800.00, which is cheap by today's standards. Her youngest brother, Justin, stayed in our motel room with us on the wedding night as he was sad because there weren't any kids his age to play with at the reception. We gathered all our gifts the next day, loaded up the Fury, and went home. We were thrilled that we had gotten $600.00 in cash gifts to help pay for almost all our remaining debt. We were on our own now—Jessie and I against the world. We didn't know what we didn't know. The world is big and has all the best players on its team. Before the ninth inning, we would look for the "mercy rule" to end the beating.

Surviving Myself

The summer seemed to fly by, and we worked hard to save every penny to go to Dallas. The old Fury started having mechanical issues sometime during the summer, so we traded it for a 1980 Pontiac Phoenix. My dad was so pissed that he could barely speak. He liked the old Fury and chastised me up one side and down the other about how easily it could have been repaired, and we wouldn't have had a car payment. My dad hated ever having anything new or like new, as it was a total waste of money. He also had the new tires on the Fury when he bought it, and we wasted that investment. My dad was always willing to point out our mistakes but never was there to offer his opinion or advice when it came time for us to make serious decisions. He figured he didn't need any help or didn't get any help from his parents, so why would his kids need any of that? It was just easier to deride us for our dumb decisions. I wasn't eager to go to him for advice.

When August arrived, we loaded all worldly possessions that would fit into our Phoenix and headed down I-35 for Dallas. I trusted the Rand McNally Atlas would be our guide and provide the best directions for how to get where we needed. The only problem was that Jessie had to read the map while I drove. It never occurred to me that she didn't understand how maps work.

On the first day, we got around Kansas City and stayed in Emporia, Kansas, hoping to make it to Dallas the next day. Things went fairly well until we arrived on the edge of the Dallas-Fort Worth Metroplex, as the radio called it. We were suddenly on a 6-lane freeway traveling at well over 70 mph to keep from getting run over. I gave Jessie instructions on what to look for on the map while trying to read all the different information and exit signs. Unfortunately, she had no idea what to look for, and at the speed we were going, it was nearly impossible to give me enough notice before our exit came around. We missed and kept heading south and deeper into the city. I finally decided to get off the freeway and took the next exit, not knowing where it would lead. We ended up near what appeared to be stockyards with train tracks running in nearly every direction. I pulled over and grabbed the atlas to see if I could make heads or tails of where we were and how we could get to where we needed to be. I thought I had a plan, gave her back the map, and started driving on the city streets, avoiding the freeway at all costs. All she had to do was call out the next set of side streets until I recognized the streets near the Dallas Theater Center. She struggled, and I turned into my father and started cussing her out and screaming until she was crying and dropped the map. We wandered around for nearly 2 hours until, by sheer luck, we landed on the correct street where the theater center was. I expected to see a huge building with a large lighted marquee outside. Instead, it was a small, artsy-looking structure much smaller than the fine arts center at Viterbo. There was no marquee, just a business-looking sign-out front saying "Dallas Theater Center." I also expected some campus surrounding the center, but it was located in a mix of residential and business properties. We stopped out front and went inside to see if I could find the director and let him know I was here. As I entered, nobody was there to greet me or give me any information. I walked further inside and found the theater itself. I ended up in the main stage's wings, and people were everywhere doing various jobs. I introduced myself to the first person I saw and asked if they could tell me where the graduate student advisor might be. When I ended the sentence, a gentleman approached me and said he was the person I was looking for. I explained that I had just arrived from Wisconsin and needed to know where the dorms were so my wife and I could settle. He told me there were no dorms and that most students found housing independently. He did offer the name and phone number of a man who rented to most of the students in the program. Then I asked when I would return and what I would do initially. He said most first-year students spend most of their time in the scene shop and do technical support for the 2nd year student productions. I didn't express my disappointment, but I thought I drove 1000 miles to do the same stuff I had been doing at Viterbo for the last four years. He said to come back on Monday, and we would get started. I left and took the information for the rental. I contacted the man, who gave me directions and met us at a duplex a few miles from the theater center. It wasn't the nicest place, but better than I had lived on Johnson

St. in LaCrosse. We decided to take it and gave him the $295.00 deposit so he would let us move in. By this time, we were so tired of traveling and the hassle of the city. We just wanted to get out of the car and settle down. We unloaded everything we had brought and headed to a nearby grocery store to get something to put in the refrigerator. It was so hot, and the apartment didn't have traditional air conditioning, but these giant louvers in the ceiling would open, and a fan would draw the heat out of the building and blow it through some system in the roof. It was loud and removed the hottest of the air but didn't replace it with any cooler air. As we arranged things in the kitchen, a few large cockroaches scooted across the floor, looking for someplace to hide. I squashed them with a loud crunch under my shoe. Jessie looked at me with a look that said I don't want to be here. We made the best of it, set up our little TV, and rolled out our blankets on the bedroom floor. We figured we could buy a bed and some furniture at a local store easier than carrying all those things in a trailer behind the car. We were both exhausted and stressed and tried our best to get some sleep. The next day, we were going to KRLD radio station in Dallas as Jessie's boss at WIZM in LaCrosse had arranged for her to interview for a job in the traffic department there. We got up the next day and again did our best to try and find the radio station. This time, we ended up on the wrong road and somehow wandered into a new subdivision under construction in Fort Worth, right next to Dallas. After a few hours of screaming, frustration, and crying, I found the radio station. We both went in, and the people were very welcoming. They offered us refreshments and then pointed out all the city of Dallas attractions. Come to find out, they were the flagship station for the Dallas Cowboys and had their suite at Arlington Stadium to watch the games. We would have the chance to go to all the Dallas Cowboys football games free of charge and enjoy food and drinks. Although we both were Viking fans and hated the Cowboys, it was exciting. They offered Jessie a job and gave her until Monday to decide if she wanted it. We left and then tried like hell to return to our apartment. By then, our phones had been turned on, and we could call home and let everyone know that we had arrived and were getting set up. After Jessie talked to her parents, she hung up the phone and started to cry. She was homesick and unsure if she could handle living so far away. I told her we would be okay and needed to get used to it. It was Friday night, and we had a couple of beers and food and then went back to bed to watch TV and sleep. The next morning, we were going to find a furniture store and get cheap chairs, a table, a couch, and a bed. We had about 750.00 dollars of the $1000.00 or so that we brought with us. As we got outside our apartment, we noticed that the car parked across the street from us had been stripped during the night. All the tires were gone, and the windows were broken out. It didn't give us the greatest feeling in the world. We tried again to venture into Dallas and find a furniture store. Once more, hours slipped away as we grappled with the familiar struggle of navigating through the city's bustling streets. Eventually, we stopped at a store, our gaze sweeping across the interior. It was apparent we weren't in the LaCrosse market. Even the junk was very expensive, and we could not buy much more than a table and chairs and a bed. We didn't buy anything and just got back in the car. It was tranquil as we made our way back to the duplex. We got back inside, and Jessie began crying again. She wanted to go home. I felt like shit for having dragged her down to this place. Like always, I decided with little or no forethought or planning. I assumed I could figure it out like I did at Viterbo, but Dallas was too big to "wing it." I also started crying and tried to comfort her while discussing what we would do. She was sure she could get her old job back at WIZM if we returned. I told her that if I left, I wouldn't be able to get another chance to try school again for another year, and I didn't want to work at the Jewelry Store for the lousy 3.40 an hour I was getting when I left. I also didn't want to let my folks down and listen to my father chew my ass for going to college and into the theater in the first place. Jessie couldn't stop crying no matter what I said, so I finally asked her if she was sure she wanted to go home and if that would make her happy. She said yes. I finally agreed. We stayed the rest of the day and planned on leaving on Monday after we had a chance to call the Dallas Theater Center and let them know I wouldn't be attending, and she could call KRLD and do the same. That night was the first night we decently slept since we had started this adventure. We packed everything back up on Sunday and loaded the car to leave on Monday. We both called home on Sunday night and told our parents we were coming home. My mother was emotional on the other end of the phone and wanted to know what happened. I said I would explain when I got back. I could hear my dad in the background cussing and saying that he had left home at 17 and made it on his own, but his college-educated son couldn't. Monday morning, Jessie called the radio station and gave them the news, and they were very kind, wishing us a safe trip home. I called the director at the theater center, and he was less than pleased with me. He said he had turned down other students, and they would be shorthanded for the school year and the upcoming production season. I apologized and explained that we weren't ready for the big city and that my wife cried nearly the entire three days we were here. He wanted me to know that if I left, I couldn't return later and try again. I understood. We called the landlord and told him we were going and that he could keep the $295.00 deposit. He was a nice fellow and said if we gave him an address, he would return the money if he found another renter soon. I said thanks, and we left the keys inside and headed north. For some reason, exiting the city was much easier than getting in. I didn't even need the atlas; in no time, Dallas was in the rearview mirror.

I would never act in another play in my life. I would never direct another play in my life. When we returned to Wisconsin, my sister in Sparta offered to let us stay in her basement until we found our place to live and get employed again. Jessie called WIZM, and they had filled the position she left already. However, they offered her a job in advertising sales with an opportunity to make 30 plus grand per year. She said yes and was able to start the following week. I didn't call the jewelry store but instead tried to find something more befitting of a college graduate. The truth was that in 1981 there was a deep recession, and the number of good jobs was far exceeded by the people seeking them. The other issue I was having took me by surprise. Many places I had applied to had never heard of Viterbo College. They also were less than impressed with my degree in Theater Arts. Now, things might have been different if I had a degree in Business Management or Accounting. After a couple of weeks, I received a letter from Jackson County Bank informing me that I needed to contact them to arrange a repayment schedule for the $5,000 of student loans I had taken. I had no idea how I would pay that back without employment.

I talked to my brother Randy about many things, including my loans, and he informed me of the loan repayment program that the National Guard was offering. My brother Randy was a 1st Lt., and my brother Jerry was a sergeant in the guard at the time. All I had to do was enlist for six years, and the guard would pay my loans and give me a $1500.00 enlistment bonus. It sounded like a good deal to me. I could make some money, get additional training, pay my loans, and shut my dad up about what an idiot I was for attending college. I talked with Jessie and told her the details.

I would be gone for about 5-6 months with basic training and AIT (Advanced Individual Training), where I would learn my specific job for the military. She said she could handle that if we found a decent living place before I left. We used the remaining money and rented the basement apartment of a new duplex in the Pfaff Subdivision just outside Sparta.

On September 11, 1981, my brother swore me into the 106th Supply and Service Company of the Wisconsin Army National Guard. I would leave two weeks later for basic training at Fort Jackson, South Carolina, known as the home of the U.S. Army Drill Sergeant School. And the DJ put on the same broken record of my life. I had no idea of what I was getting into.

Chapter Thirteen:

Drill and Ceremony

The plane landed in Columbia, South Carolina, and I got off, found the baggage claim, and then looked for the bus that would take recruits from the airport to Fort Jackson. Once they had 50 riders, the bus would leave and head for the fort. We arrived through the main gate, and after a couple of turns, we were told to unload at the Fort Jackson Reception Center. This is where recruits were staged and prepared to be assigned to their companies and platoons. Countless young men were milling around, talking and smoking cigarettes.

As I walked toward the front of the building, there was a sign indicating where new arrivals should report. I went inside and reported to the desk. The private behind the desk found my name on a list, checked me in, and told me to hang out until I was called. I went back outside and found a place to sit with the others until my name was called. After about an hour, a sergeant blew a whistle and told everyone to pay attention. He read off a bunch of names and told those people to gather in an area to his right. I was among them. He then led the group to another building, where we went inside and were assigned lockers to put our belongings in. Once that was done, we formed a column of two and walked into another building. We were given haircuts and issued our uniforms, underwear, boots, and other gear, including a large duffle bag. We were told to put all our issued items into the duffle bag and then walk back to the original area to gather our belongings from the lockers.

After that, we waited for further instructions. Not long after that, a vehicle that looked like a cross between a school bus and a trolley car pulled up. It had two sets of double doors on the side front and back. It was olive green in color with no markings of any kind. The front door opened, and a tall, thin man in a Class A uniform exited and walked past the group and into the building. A few minutes later, he came out and addressed the group. As he called your name, you were to grab everything and get aboard the vehicle. I heard my name and got on board. To my surprise, the vehicle had no individual seats but a series of benches, two running back-to-back down the center and one each outside. As we sat down, we were told to put our duffle bag and belongings on our lap to make room for everyone.

It was sweltering inside, and as more people boarded, we were forced to sit so close to each other as we were touching. We were packed in like cattle and later discovered these vehicles were affectionately named "Cattle Cars." Guys were talking and started trying to figure out what would happen next. I sat silently, feeling that nobody knew what was about to happen. When the last man boarded, the thin man came aboard, the doors were closed, and the vehicle began to move. The tall, thin man stood silently at the front of the bus, holding onto a pole. We drove to another part of the fort far from the reception center.

Looking out the window, I could see row after row of 3-story brick buildings passing by with various number groups and nomenclature on each. The bus stopped, and the tall, thin man exited the vehicle, leaving us to sit and wait. He disappeared, walking up a sidewalk around the corner of the building we were parked by. Some 15 minutes later, the tall, thin man came into full view again on the sidewalk dressed in camouflage full-duty uniform with shiny black boots and the signature drill sergeant hat. It was the same man that had left earlier. The doors of the bus opened, and he climbed into the vehicle. He wasn't quiet anymore.

Surviving Myself

In a thunderous authoritative voice, he screamed for us to get our good-for-nothing asses out of his vehicle now. He then grabbed duffle bags and suitcases and threw them out the bus door. He was hollering to hurry with a series of expletives describing what he thought of us. People began to move with a purpose, and all the smiles were gone from every face. As I got to the door, my suitcase got stuck in the entry, and before I could release it, he grabbed it from me and tossed it some 20 yards onto the lawn, upon which the latch broke, and everything inside spilled out. As I tried to gather it, he screamed to leave it and get my ass to the platoon area around the corner.

We were assembled on a concrete floor covered by the barracks we were about to occupy. The first thing he did was arrange us by height in 4 rows/columns from front to back and left to right. This would be our formation. We learned basic drill and ceremony orders like standing at attention, parade rest, and at ease. He insisted we stand tall and face forward without looking directly at him unless instructed. Those who didn't follow that simple command were put into the push-up position and made to do 25 push-ups while counting out loud, "One sergeant; two sergeant," and so on until they reached 25 and were ordered to return to attention. Failing to count meant starting over, and failing to say sergeant after each number also meant starting over.

Soon, we were ordered to take our items up the stairwell to the 3rd floor, change into our uniforms, and stow all the rest away in a locker next to a bunk. We had five minutes to do this; four minutes were already gone by the time he yelled the order. I ran back out to the yard, collected my belongings, and then ran up the stairs with that and my duffle bag. As I entered the sleeping area, there were two bays with 15 bunk beds and lockers on each side. On one end was a day room with tables, pay phone, and television. On the other was a large locker room-style bath and shower area. I grabbed a locker, started getting dressed and put my items inside a locker when the sergeant entered to let us know we were too slow. He screamed for us to get back downstairs to the platoon area. I finished dressing, threw my stuff in the locker, and ran downstairs. We returned to formation, dropped as a group, and started doing push-ups.

Sergeant First Class (SFC) Murphy had gotten our attention and informed us that he would be our mother, father, grandma, and grandpa for the next eight weeks, and we better get used to it. SFC Murphy was about 6'2 and weighed around what I guessed to be 170 lbs. He was nothing but muscle from head to toe and moved deliberately with great agility and, if needed, athletic quickness. He had served in Vietnam and knew what happened to soldiers who didn't pay attention and weren't serious about their training. He was no one to trifle with, and even though he wasn't allowed to touch you physically, he gave the clear impression that if tested by anyone physically, he would oblige. He intimidated even the biggest soldier standing in front of him, and nobody entertained the idea of doing anything other than following orders. We continued the rest of the day learning close order drills, how and who to salute, and basic marching moves for a formation moving to the left or right. The most practiced move of the day was a half-left face followed by a front-leaning rest position. Then, we would do push-ups as a group over and over again. There are two elements to every command. The first was the preparatory command, followed by the execution command. The drill sergeant's voice always raises in pitch and volume with the preparatory command to help the soldier know who, where, what, or how of the coming execution command. There is typically a small pause, and then the command for execution takes place. Group commands must be done in unison or repeated until the company learns. Failure to master this quickly leads to the push-up routine mentioned above. This was repeated over and over this day, with the only breaks coming for the evening meal and smoke breaks.

Before being dismissed for the evening, we were told that the lights out time was at 2030 hrs. Sgt. Murphy also informed us that there would be duties assigned to individuals each day and night of basic training. Those are KP (kitchen police), meaning working in the mess hall and fire guard in the barracks. Someone will be awake every two hours and patrolling the barracks to ensure no fires. At the end of his shift, the soldier will wake the next fire guard and so on throughout the night until 0430 hrs waking up the following day. Rank fills alphabetically duty rosters. This means starting with last names beginning with A and so on to last names beginning with Z. Those with the highest rank are first down to the lower ranks. My college degree paid off because they gave me the rank of Private First Class or PFC, the highest private ranking. Therefore, I was first on the list in my platoon on the duty roster. The next day, I was told to report to the mess hall at 0430 for KP.

The fireguard awakened me at 0400 and I did my best to get dressed and report to the mess hall by 0430. Several other soldiers were reporting as well. This battalion mess hall served approximately 4,000 troops three meals a day. The mess sergeant was a large black man who looked like an NFL offensive lineman. He was dressed in an all-white duty uniform with shiny brass insignia on his collars and a white cook's hat. He took our names, told us to get a tray, and then gave us breakfast. We had 15 minutes to eat and then report to him for our duties. As my luck continued, I was assigned what he called pots and pans. For the next 14 hours, a kid from Pennsylvania and I would do nothing but scrub pots and pans in a 3-bay stainless steel sink. They inspected every item for cleanliness, and any item not passing would have to be washed again, often including a dry scrubbing compound and a scouring pad.

We worked nearly every minute of the day until 1900 hrs with only 15-minute breaks for lunch and supper. When we finished, my hands were red, wrinkled, raw, and throbbing. I was exhausted and looking forward to returning to the barracks for a shower and sleep. When I got to my locker, I found my bunk completely dismantled and my bedding thrown into a pile. My bunkmate told me I had not made the bunk correctly when I left that morning, so Sgt. Murphy tore it up. Thankfully, my bunk mate helped me and showed me the prescribed way Sgt. Murphy wanted the bunk made every day. I put it together, headed for the showers, and jumped into bed to relax for a few minutes before lights out.

I took the picture of Jessie from my wallet and stared at it, wondering how she was doing. I missed her and couldn't wait to get through this and back home. I put the picture under the springs of the top bunk above me so I could look at it first thing every morning and last thing every night. The next eight weeks were going to be difficult, but I survived and graduated into the next phase of training AIT (Advanced Individual Training), which meant riding a bus to Fort Gordon, GA. I was in the best shape of my life, going from 198 lbs when I arrived at Ft. Jackson, to 177 lbs on the last day of basic training. I had become the standard army's version of a "lean, mean fighting machine" who could "chew barbed wire and spit nails." I missed home and missed Jessie terribly except for a few phone calls; we only communicated by letters that came about once a week. One nice thing was that I was making about $1000.00 per month with dependent pay and was able to send home $950.00 of it. Nothing genuinely worth spending money on in training.

After basic training, my orders were to go to Ft. Gordon, Georgia. I arrived at Fort Gordon and reported to Bravo company per my orders. Every six weeks, a new class for my MOS (military occupational specialty) 72E10 Combat Telecommunications Center Operator starts. I ended up in a room with six other guys on the second floor of the 3-story barracks.

It was more like a dorm room than what we had in basic training. There were three white guys and three black guys in our room. A kid named Steve from Iowa and I were in the National Guard while the other four guys were in the regular army. It was pretty much like going to college, except that we had to fall in for formation every morning at 0700 hrs and then march to the classroom or the field, depending on where our training was taking place. We were given an hour for lunch, where we could go to the mess hall and then return. Class ended at around 1500 hrs, and from there, we marched to the parade grounds for group PT (Physical Training). After that, we marched back to the barracks and were excused for the evening unless there was an inspection or the company was assigned a GI party. A GI party meant everyone was to clean every barracks area from top to bottom and then stand for inspection. I enjoyed having the evenings free, and we were allowed to change out of our duty uniforms unless we had extra duty like fire guard etc. After eating, I would go to the day room to watch TV or play pool at night. One night a week, I would wash my clothes. As many times as I could, I would call home.

There were only two pay phones in the barracks, so it was a crap shoot as to when you could get a chance to use them. Sometimes, Steve and I would walk to the PX (Post Exchange) to buy something or to the post restaurant for a meal. It was a nice change from the mess hall or the vehicles visiting the field to serve coffee or drinks. They looked like the food trucks you would see at the county fair, but the food was nothing like those. We called them the "roach coach" or "maggot wagon" but ate from them anyway.

Most Combat Telecommunications Center Operator training centered on learning how to type on a teletype machine. It differed from a typewriter in that it only had three rows of keys. It produced a tape that could be fed into a machine to send the message to someone with the same machine on the other end. The tape was the same as those ticker tapes you would see in the movies with stock information. It was a paper tape, and the holes punched in the tape represented the letters of the teletype machine. This system used what was called the Baudot code. It was similar to what the old IBM computers used in their punch card system. It was pretty clever, but even in 1981, it was considered old technology. These teletype machines were mounted in commo vans that contained radios, phones, and encryption machines that would scramble the signals sent so the enemy couldn't intercept any messaging.

By the time we reached the end of the training, the Army had already developed a replacement machine called the UGC-74, which was a typewriter with memory. It was the precursor to the computer. When I returned to the 106th in Black River, they had an old teletype machine from WWII that nobody had ever taken out of the box. The real joke was that one teletype machine is useless unless you have someone on the other end who also has one. So here I trained for eight weeks to use a piece of equipment that will never be used again in an actual combat situation: only me and only the U. S. Army. I became skilled in communication with radio operations, field phones, and switchboard operations like "Radar" on M*A*S*H.

A few years later, I would receive a letter of commendation for training the Group and Battalion Communications Sergeants and

Officers on operating their teletypes and setting up an actual field training exercise using them for the first time in their history. After that exercise, the teletypes were returned to the boxes and never used again. In the six-plus years I served in the Wisconsin Army National Guard, I would earn another two stripes and become a Sgt. E-5, usually called a Buck Sgt. I was encouraged by the company commander to consider becoming an officer and taking the exam for officer candidate school. I took it and scored one of the highest scores they had ever seen. With a lot of pressure, I went to the Wisconsin Military Academy at Camp Douglas. Once again, I wasn't prepared for what was going to happen. The first two days were a repeat of basic training only on steroids. After no sleep and rolling around in the gravel parking lot, I failed to see what this had to do with becoming a leader of men. So I left much to the chagrin of my brother, who had gone through the program years before, and my father, who once again questioned what the hell I was doing. There is only so much I was willing to put myself through to make others happy. Repeating the physical demands of basic training at 26 wasn't one of them. I returned to my unit and served with distinction until honorably discharged in 1989. I am not sorry for my military experience. It taught me a lot about discipline, honor, duty, and camaraderie.

I wish I had enlisted or attended one of the academies right out of high school. It did what I asked it to do, pay my student loans. I made some lifelong friends and have some great memories from my service. The only thing it couldn't do was help with the struggles Jessie and I were having.

Chapter Fourteen:

If At First

I returned home in the spring of 1981 and got my job back at Cremer Jewelers. Now, I would be a salesman working for an hourly rate and a small commission on sales. Jessie continued at the radio station and was doing pretty well in advertising sales. Our lives were uneventful as we worked during the week and on the weekends. We usually returned to the Millville farm to spend time with her parents and siblings. Of course, drinking and playing cards were the order of the day on most visits. Occasionally, we would float down the Zumbro River or visit her grandma. The kids often asked us to pick them up because Jack was being mean and noisy or arguing and tossing stuff at Mary until the sheriffs arrived due to the trouble at home. We would load the kids in the car and bring them back to our house, or sometimes our presence would settle the situation down, and things went back to "normal." We worked hard but never really had any extra money after our bills. We were young, and despite everything, it felt like we were close to each other and counted on each other "for better or worse," as the vow goes. I was working my way up the ladder at the store, and Mr. Cremer wanted me to learn to do jewelry appraisal work. He was one of only 50 certified gemologists in the jewelry industry at the time. He taught me a great deal about colored gemstones, gold, and mostly diamond grading. I learned how to use a micrometer and measure diamonds for quality of cut dimensions, master diamonds and a diamond lite for measuring color, and a 10x diamond scope to determine clarity. I wasn't certified, but Mr. Cremer approved my work, which was good enough for me. I would continue to do appraisal work for years and expand into pearls and other materials like jade or lapis lazuli. It was fascinating and eventually helped me when I became a manager and buyer. Things were relatively routine until 1984. That year, Jessie and I were expecting our first child. I approached old man Cremer for a raise, hoping to help ease the anticipated extra expense of raising a child. I was making a whopping $3.40 an hour plus about $150 in commissions a month. I asked for .25 cents an hour, and he acted as I asked for his first-born child. He then went on to tell me that if he gave me a raise, he would have to give everyone a raise, and he couldn't afford to do it. This is from a man who owned a home in one of the most exclusive areas of LaCrosse and another in California. I would hate for him not to be able to pay his $1200/month membership to the LaCrosse Country Club as well. So, I continued working and looking for another opportunity to increase my income. The early 80s was not exactly in a boom. Then, one day, I answered an ad in the local paper from the Federal Government looking for young men with military experience for openings within the Department of Treasury. I was young and had military experience, so I answered the ad. To my surprise, it was recruitment for the Secret Service. I had no idea the Secret Service was under the Department of Treasury. So, I completed a rather lengthy application and provided a number of references. I heard nothing for about two months and figured nothing would happen.

As I was about to give up hope, I received an official government letter. I was congratulated for passing their initial background check. The letter also included a number to call to schedule a face-to-face meeting with the Secret Service Director's Office Operations in Madison, Wisconsin. I called and arranged a meeting at the office in Madison. I was super excited and nervous at the same time. The office was located in a tall building on Wilson Street in Madison. The building also housed many other state and federal agencies. I arrived at the Secret Service office and was let in through several locked doors and finally to the DOO's office.

The Director Operations Manager was a middle-aged man with thinning gray hair, a round belly, glasses, and a pleasing smile. He looked like someone's favorite uncle. He was wearing a white shirt, tie, dress slacks, black shoes, and, most notably, a shoulder holster with some kind of pistol neatly tucked in. He shook my hand, introduced himself as Dale Keaner, and asked me to sit across from his desk. The chairs were large and comfortable, and his office was elegant, with all kinds of pictures on his desk and the walls. Most were black and white, and I recognized several presidents, including John F. Kennedy, Lyndon Johnson, and Richard Nixon. There were also all kinds of letters and framed commendations. He started the interview by telling me that this was the first step in becoming an agent for the Department of Treasury, specifically the Secret Service. He explained that they had already done a preliminary background check on me with many different people in my life, including teachers, military superiors, and others. They reviewed all my education records from grade school through college. They knew about my family, especially my father, who was in the service. They knew how many siblings I had and that my mother was a nurse. The background results were very positive, and the fact that I had a top-secret security clearance with the U.S. Army was a bonus. We discussed various subjects, and it didn't feel anything like an interview. We talked politics, and he told me about his experiences as the head of security at the White House during the Lyndon Johnson presidency. He had traveled the world many times and especially enjoyed visiting Australia. He went on to explain that new agents did the most physically demanding duties, such as running alongside a motorcade and standing in crowds for hours during speeches, parades, and other events. They also did the most traveling. He also said that not all the Secret Service did was protect the president, but they also investigated criminal activity, including counterfeiting bank robbery, and fraud. He then told me that training for agents would take place at Quantico in Virginia and was in conjunction with those recruits for the FBI and CIA. He said it would be stressful and challenging; the new agents spent little time at home. They always had a packed bag and a plane ticket good to anywhere in the world at a moment's notice. He then asked me if I was still interested. If so, the next step in the process would be to take the entrance exam. It would be scheduled for another time and taken at the federal office in Milwaukee. He said the entrance exam takes approximately 4-6 hours. He was satisfied with our interview and recommended that I advance to the next step. We shook hands, and I left. I was on cloud nine when I told Jessie that maybe I had finally found the right opportunity for me that would be a career and offer enough pay and benefits that we would never have to worry. She was also excited, and we waited for the next phone call. The call came, and I headed to Milwaukee to take the test. The offices were once again heavily secured and required providing ID through a bank-type window before being buzzed in. In this case, I was escorted to what must have been their conference room. It had the biggest table I had ever seen and was surrounded by at least 30 chairs. There was a wall of windows along one side. The agent conducting the test offered me coffee or water if needed and asked if I needed to use the restroom. Once the test began, I could not leave the room for any reason. I passed on the water but used the restroom and then returned. He officially told me the test was beginning and handed me two black and white photos of early 1950 street scenes. He told me to look at them carefully, and he would return in 10 minutes. No further explanation. He returned and took the photos from me and then gave me a test booklet and answer sheet like a college entrance exam. There were sections on English, Math, and History with multiple-choice questions. Fill in the circle stuff. This portion of the test took about two hours to complete. Then he returned to the room and gave me another booklet of stories of crime investigations that then asked a series of questions to determine decision-making. Then, there was a logic booklet with puzzles asking for conclusions based on the information given. Finally, the last section of the test was on recall. A series of about 50 questions asked for details within the pictures he had given me at the beginning. For instance, what time was it on the clock in the jewelry store window? Which direction was the pick-up truck facing? What was the license number on the black sedan parked in front of the clothing store? These questions went on and on, and I had only 30 minutes to complete this section. He returned, collected the materials, and told me I must have a 90% or more score to continue the process. Once again, they would be contacting me. He also told me that candidates from Illinois and Minnesota would also be taking the exam. If they had more candidates pass than openings available, the top scores would get preference. I thanked him and left with my head spinning. I had never taken a test like that before, and it was difficult, interesting, and challenging. I thought I did okay, but wasn't sure about scoring 90% or more. I was on pins and needles waiting to hear and daydreaming about what it would be like to be a "secret agent." About three weeks later, I received a letter from the Department of the Treasury. Inside were the results of the test I had taken. I scored a 93% and passed. I was given a phone number to call to arrange the final interview, which was to take place at the Everett Dirksen Federal Building in Chicago. I was so excited that I could barely sleep at night. Jessie and I decided to go to Chicago together the day before the interview to avoid the disaster I had for my auditions in college. We stayed at the Holiday Inn downtown. I was able to walk to the Dirksen Building and took the elevator up to the 20th floor. There were no other offices on that floor except those for the Secret Service. Again, I was in the entry lobby and figured I would have to go through several locked doors to meet the agent in charge of conducting the interview. Instead, after letting the receptionist know I was there, a tall black man in a gray suit with a white shirt and red tie came into the lobby to greet me. He escorted me back to another conference room filled with men and women agents sitting around the huge table. They all had their shoulder holsters on or draped over the back of their chairs. They looked like regular people of all shapes, sizes, and colors. He told me that I was one of only four people who had passed the exam in the three states they gave it. He also said they had finished all their background investigations on me, and as far as they were concerned, I would make a great candidate for the service. Then he said something that totally surprised me. He said today's interview aims to talk me out of becoming a secret service agent. I sat at the table, and one by one, each agent at the table told me of their experiences within the agency. It was very sobering. Most had traveled to multiple countries around the world. They said they had spent many weeks away from home without knowing when they might return. As rewarding as their work was, it came at a high price. Virtually everyone there had been divorced at least once and struggled to maintain a normal family life. Due to the demands of the job, they moved from city to city many different times. The agent in charge finished the repeated recounting of the story and then told me it was up to me to make the decision. They would be spending over 100 thousand dollars on my training. I would go to Quantico for 12 weeks and then be assigned to a field office to begin on-the-job training. He then told me to call my wife and make her aware of what the agents had presented to me. After that call, he wanted me to answer them yes or no. So, he put me in a private room with a telephone, and I called Jessie at the hotel to talk. I explained everything I had heard and needed to know how she felt. I would be gone a lot, and with her expecting our first child, I wasn't sure how much help I would be. She would be the one who maintained our household, and I would be sending home a decent amount of money each month. The truth of the matter was that we just weren't sure how strong our relationship was. The time I was away at basic training was challenging, but we knew it would have an end. The longer we talked, the more scared we became about possibly losing our marriage. As the realization hit me that I would not accept this opportunity, I had that same sick feeling I had in the past. This was it. It was likely my last chance to escape the jewelry store and do something out of the ordinary with my life. I told Jessie goodbye and would be there after I told them I declined the offer. I hung up the phone, and the door opened nearly as soon as I did. It was the agent in charge. He closed the door behind himself and said, "Jay, you made the right decision. Do not be upset. We would have liked to have you as a member of the agency, but it's clear your family is more important."

I fought back the tears in my eyes. He told me they had listened to the phone call, which was part of the final evaluation. He wished me well and congratulated me on getting this far in the process. I told him thank you, and I was sorry for taking up their time. He again reassured me that it was no problem and that they had gone through this many times with other candidates. As we drove home from Chicago, I couldn't help but feel like I had made another mistake. I justified my actions, knowing that I loved my wife and didn't want to be away from my children in the future. The funny thing is that I regret this decision more than not pursuing my graduate assistantship. Well, regret is the song sung by those who live a life without calling upon God for guidance—next verse.

Chapter Fifteen:

Blessings and Burdens

O n May 5, 1984, the 106th Supply and Service Company of Black River Falls, WI, was departing for Giessen, Germany, for annual training. I was a Spec 4 in the headquarters section with responsibilities for communications and assisting as the unit supply sergeant. We flew commercial air to an air base in New Jersey and then boarded a MAC (Military Air Charter) flight for Rhein-Main Air Base near Frankfurt, Germany. It was a 13-hour non-stop flight. In addition to our company, many civilian dependents and other military personnel were on board. We landed around 1300 hrs the next day and boarded military buses to drive to Giessen. When we arrived, it was nice to find that all of our tents and equipment had been set up so we could unpack our gear and take some time to shake off the jet lag and familiarize ourselves with the area. We all slept hard that night. The next morning, I was summoned to our headquarters tent. When I arrived, a young woman from the Red Cross was waiting for me and delivered the message that my wife had given birth to a girl. It was May 7, 1984, and my daughter, Teren, arrived a little early. The lady from the Red Cross had a few details, like what hospital Jessie was in and the phone number to call. She told me the only place on the post with a pay phone was the *bundespost* (German Federal Post). I had to calculate the time difference to ensure I did not call in the middle of the night. I told my brothers and tent mates the news, and everyone was very excited and supportive. The hard part was knowing I was stuck there for the next 13 days before I could get home and see her. I made my way to the post office and called Jessie. She was excited and said Lynne had come to help her through the birth. Teren was having trouble eating, and they suspected that she had a milk allergy. She would be staying in the hospital for another three days until they determined the best formula to feed her. I was anxious for the next two weeks and spent some $80 on phone calls and another $40 on a German Cabbage Patch doll to take home to her. When we returned after training, we landed in LaCrosse at about 0100 hrs in the morning. The guys on the plane allowed me to be the first one off, and I double-timed it from the aircraft to the airport lobby. Jessie was there with Teren in her arms. I hugged them both hard, took Teren in my arms, and stared at how beautiful she was. I could barely see through the tears in my eyes. I also told Jessie how much I loved her and how proud I was of her for going through this without me. The three of us jumped into our car and drove home to Sparta. I stayed up the whole night with Teren laying between us, just thankful I got home ok and she was alright. From then on, I was more determined than ever to work as hard as possible at the jewelry store and do everything I could to take care of my family. Jessie was doing well at the radio station and making good money. I sensed her feeling a confidence that she hadn't had before. She was also expressing herself more and seeking a little more independence to do things independently without always confiding in me. Occasionally, it would lead to some disputes, usually about spending money on something she wanted but was not the best for the family. She argued that she made the most money and should have more say in spending it. I tried to tell her that we needed to save some money for a rainy day and possibly have enough to buy a house someday. She insisted that we needed a newer vehicle because her work required that she have dependable transportation and a nicer vehicle that would give clients confidence in her success. She also upgraded her wardrobe and personal appearance via expensive hair salon appointments for the same reasons. Hence, we never had a savings account and typically lived paycheck to paycheck, hoping nothing would go wrong. Jessie was a good mother when it came to caring for Teren. She did all the tasks mothers generally would do with excellent efficiency. I was a little upset that she felt the need to go back to work and not spend more time off with our new baby but there wasn't any family medical or paid maternity leave back then, so our bank account wouldn't fill itself. I thought having children would bring us closer together, and when we were all together in the same space, it felt that way.

However, when Teren was not with us, I started to feel like Jessie had her own relationship with Teren and my own relationship with Teren. It is kind of like we weren't on the same page. We just kept plugging away, and eventually, I would become the assistant manager at Cremer's and enjoy a decent increase in pay. Not long after that, Jessie decided she wanted to apply for a job in sales at KTTC-TV in Rochester, MN. It was closer to her folks; she thought it was more money and prestigious than radio sales. She got the job, so we needed to find a place closer to Rochester. We settled in a newer three-bedroom townhouse in Eyota, MN, just 10 miles east of Rochester on I-90. For the next two years, I'll drive back to LaCrosse for work, embarking on my journey at 8:00 in the morning. My return will depend on my shift at the store; I'll head back home at either 6:00 PM after completing the 9:00 to 5:00 shift or at 10:00 PM if I'm on the 9:00 to 9:00 shift. I worked either Saturday or Sunday every week as well. On my off weekends, I would drive back to Black River to attend my National Guard drills to fulfill that obligation.

There were many months that I ended up working 30 days straight. It was kind of ironic when I passed on some opportunities in my life because I did not want to be away from my family. Jessie felt successful in her television sales career and often bragged (and exaggerated) to her siblings about the workings of television and how she knew the local TV personalities. She also had more evening events in conjunction with her work and needed one of her sisters or mother to babysit Teren until she was done or I could get home. We were leading separate lives in one sense, and it manifested itself in more arguments, less family time, and fewer intimate connections as a couple. Then Jessie became pregnant again, and we were expecting our next child in February 1986. I hoped we would have a boy and our family would be complete.

Jessie struggled with pregnancy and did not have the same optimism or the "motherly glow" that came with our first child. I worked harder, tried to support her more than before, and forgave some of her indulgences with money. Ethan was born on February 28th, and I was there through the entire process, even being able to cut the umbilical cord in the delivery room. Teren was thrilled to have a baby brother to love, hold, and give kisses to. I was concerned for Jessie, however, as she was less connected to Ethan than she was to Teren, and although she fulfilled her motherly duties, she seemed almost upset that she now had another baby to care for. I thought it might be postpartum depression and expressed to her that she should talk to a doctor about it. She was angry at me for the suggestion and didn't feel the need to pursue anything. She just needed some time for herself and maybe a few more nights out with friends to relax. Her occasional drink to relax now and then became a nightly ritual. It worked because she seemed easier to get along with after her after-work brandy, but one would become two, and the glass kept getting larger. I often had a beer after work but never made it mandatory to get through the night. Within six months of Ethan's birth, we moved to Plainview and rented a newer three-bedroom ranch house in a newly developed subdivision. The house owner was trying to get us to buy it on a land contract with a thousand dollars down. He wanted 45,000.00 for the home, which seemed like a million to us then. We could not come up with the 1,000.00 for the down payment anyway, and I knew Jessie's folks didn't have it. I asked my dad for it and got nothing but a lecture about how he made it on his own without a college education and so on, and so on, until I felt like shit for even asking. My mother would have given it if she did not have to live with my father after having done so. My dad was not into sympathy or charity. He often said that sympathy is in the dictionary between shit and syphilis. We could afford the 400.00 a month rent and brandy. What else should I expect?

We hadn't lived there very long before Jessie surprised me by saying one day that she wasn't sure she loved me anymore and that maybe we should consider separating for a while. I was stunned and not sure what to say. I asked what happened. Did I do something? She vaguely answered that it wasn't me; it was her. Then I asked if there was someone else. She denied anything like that but wasn't happy and that she and I didn't get to spend much time together anymore. I told her it was because I had to drive to LaCrosse every day, and she was busy at work, too. So after a few more minutes of conversation, I told her I would try to get a job in Rochester at Lasker Jewelers so I wouldn't be gone so long every day and could be home earlier. It would also make it easier for me to be available to get the kids from daycare and help at home with them after supper. Maybe we would not be so tired and could spend more time together. She agreed to see if that would make a difference. Within a few weeks, I was offered a sales position with Lasker Jewelers in downtown Rochester for $6.00 per hour plus a 3% commission. So, I accepted, leaving behind Cremer Jewelers, where I had worked my way up to management and a decent salary of $19,000 a year, hoping my marriage and family would be stronger. Initially, it felt like we were doing better. Money, however, was getting tighter, and it was becoming apparent that we couldn't afford to live in the Plainview house much longer.

In addition, Jessie had become pregnant again, and the doctor indicated she was going to have twins. I thought about getting another part-time job, so I applied to be a bartender at the local golf course restaurant. I got the job, which paid $4.50 per hour plus gratuities. I went there a couple of nights a week after work until closing at 11 PM on weekdays or 1 AM on weekends. I would not say I liked it because I was usually tired and really not interested in listening to drunks and breathing in 2 or 3 packs of cigarettes a night. Jessie then told me that she thought there was something wrong with her pregnancy. She said she didn't feel right and something must be wrong with the babies. Eventually, she told me that the doctor confirmed her suspicions and that the babies were not healthy and probably deformed. She told me that he recommended she terminate the pregnancy as the children likely wouldn't survive. I was devastated by the news and didn't understand what we would do. Jessie then told me that she wanted an abortion and that she had scheduled one at a clinic in Minneapolis. I wanted to discuss this further, but she had already decided. I was struggling with how we could claim to be Catholic and entirely against abortion and decide to go ahead with not just one but two! Jessie would tell everyone who knew she was pregnant that she had a miscarriage. I didn't comment to anyone about what really had happened. Of all the things I had messed up in my life and the hurts I may have inflicted, I could never overcome the guilt of aborting our children. It felt wrong, no matter the justification. It also put a big question mark in my heart and mind about my wife. She seemed to get over this without any regret or guilt. This wasn't the same girl who took our wedding vows. Had she changed that much, or had I been blinded by my devotion to her and my desire for a family? I was bewildered and desperate to fix our marriage. It was like wanting to learn to water ski. The harder I tried, the worse I got, and the longer I held onto the rope, the more lake water I swallowed. At some point, I had to either get up on my skis or let go of the rope.

Chapter Sixteen:

Go East Young Man

As the money grew tight, we moved into the income-based rental quadruplex in Elgin, MN. I traded my Nissan Sentra for a less expensive, older 77 Mercury Grand Marquis. Having a car saved me from a monthly payment of $185.00. Although it was not as fuel-efficient, I no longer commuted 120 miles daily for work, which made the higher fuel consumption seem negligible. The $400 monthly rent went down to $295 per month, but we were cramped in a two-bedroom apartment with no garage.

Jessie was still happy because she had a new Ford Taurus station wagon to drive, costing us $360 per month, but it kept her image up as a successful sales agent. I was doing all right at Lasker's and enjoyed not having to work every weekend and no nights. It made it much easier to care for the kids and saved us from having one of Jessie's sisters babysit, waiting for me to come home from work if Jessie had a function. It appears we had finally settled back down, ready for life to resume its normal rhythm, whatever that might entail. However, Jessie would trade our Taurus Wagon (without consulting me) for a new Merkur Scorpio from one of her car dealer clients within the next year. This bumped our monthly payment to nearly $500 and got us a sports car to try and fit our family into. She loved it because it was stylish and could reach 180 mph. I failed to see the need for such a toy, not to mention it had Pirelli racing tires that were great for dry new pavement but lousy in snow and rough roads, which we traveled often. The car rode like a lumber wagon unless you were at 80 mph, at which time the suspension would respond.

I tried to talk to Jessie about not spending our money on what I thought were extravagant things like that car, and she went off. Who was I to tell her what to do? Besides, she made more money than I did. Apparently, I didn't understand how important it was for her to have a car like that for work, and, besides, she got a good deal on it because the dealership owner really liked her. I was trying to accept how her success made her life more glamorous but our family's lives less stable. There was also a definite change in our relationship as husband and wife. She treated me more like her roommate than her husband. She was sharing all kinds of gossip about her work, who was cheating on each other, and the politics within the office with a new sales manager. We didn't share our feelings about each other anymore and rarely shared intimate moments. It made me anxious and paranoid about Jessie, what was happening at her work, and the after-hours "functions" she needed to attend. I do know that there was always some drinking involved, and she would tell of the flirtations of her newfound friend Candace, who had just been divorced.

Candace had her eye on one of the married sales associates in the office. Jim was the captain/coach of the KTTC men's softball team on which I was asked to play. He seemed like a nice enough fellow. He had an attractive wife and a couple of young kids, just like we did. Why he would be interested in Candace was beyond me. In fact, I had never heard or seen him do anything with her that made me think they were anything but coworkers. Outside of those softball games, I had no friends to do anything with. It didn't matter because I had no extra time or money to do anything else anyway. I concentrated on spending time with kids as much as possible, except going to the park or taking them sledding in the winter. Of course, we continued to take them down to the farm so Grandma Mary and Grandpa Jack could see them along with their aunts and uncles. Not much had changed there. Our routine involved enjoying dinner, playing cards, sipping drinks, and finally engaging in the inevitable argument that served as our cue to head home.

Things just kept going this way until 1988. I had to make a decision as to whether I was going to re-enlist in the National Guard. I chose a two-year enlistment as I needed the money and had reached a rank where I wasn't taking as many orders as I was giving. It also gave me a reason to return to Black River and see my parents and brothers. Shortly after this, Jessie returned and told me she was tired of working at KTTC, so she applied for a General Sales Manager position at a television station in Parkersburg, West Virginia. This would be a big promotion for her; she would be in charge of the sales staff and second in charge of the station, just under the general manager. She got the job and would need to be there within 30 days to begin working. So her plan was for me to stay with the kids, and she would go down there first to start working and find a place for us to live. Once she was established, the kids and I would come down. She took off in her Merkur Scorpio two weeks later for WTAP-TV Parkersburg, leaving me and the kids in Elgin. I continued working at Lasker's and had Jessie's sisters take turns coming to the house to watch the kids if needed until I got home. After being down there for a week, she found a house to rent in Marietta, OH, just across the Ohio River from Parkersburg. So, the plan was to hire a moving company at the station's expense to move our belongings from Elgin to Marietta. It would be another 2-3 weeks before a truck was available. In the meantime, Jessie flew back to Minneapolis and picked up the kids to fly back with her to Ohio, and I would stay in Elgin, continuing to work at Lasker's and then come down once the movers had come. I decided to sell my Mercury. Instead of driving down to Ohio, I decided to fly. The vehicle had a lot of miles on it, and I wasn't sure it would make the nearly thousand-mile trip. It was difficult saying goodbye to the kids, and I was surprised at the amount of anxiety I had when I returned home alone. I had trouble sleeping and concentrating now that my routine had changed dramatically. I was also worried about them being down there without me. Jessie could certainly care for them regarding daily needs, but who would they play with or snuggle on the couch to watch a movie? She had always left those times to me while she mixed her nightly brandy, read romance novels, or talked on the phone with her mom, sisters, or Candace. The movers finally set a date, so it was time for me to give Laskers my notice. I had no employment waiting for me in Ohio. I would have to beat the streets and hope to find something once I arrived. Jessie's folks gave me a ride to Minneapolis to catch my flight to Columbus, Ohio, where Jessie and the kids would pick me up at the airport. When I arrived, the kids came running and shouting Daddy! I picked them up and squeezed them tight. It had only been a few weeks, but I missed them terribly. Jessie gave me a welcome hug and a small peck on the lips as if to say I'm glad you are here for the kid's sake. We grabbed my bags and loaded into the car for the two-plus hour drive to Marietta. As we headed southeast of Columbus, the landscape went from farm fields to rolling foothills, moving up and down from creek bottoms to hilltops. It was extremely foggy and worsened every time we went into another valley. There were few farms anymore but small, rather impoverished-looking cabins, shacks, or mobile homes scattered about in random patches. The road was rarely straight and made it difficult to discern our destination. Occasionally, we would pass through a small group of houses with some stores, a post office with a sign indicating the town's name, and a gas station. They all showed their age and gave me the impression that we were in Appalachia. After more than a few hours, we turned almost straight east and descended a winding hill down to the bottom, revealing a more modern and straight four-lane highway heading north and south alongside the Ohio River. The river was wide and flowed swiftly to the south. The water was chocolate in color and had no scenic quality. I noticed no birds or wildlife like you might along the Mississippi but only a lot of dead marsh grass and barren trees bordering its banks. A smell in the air penetrated the car's interior, like that of a catalytic converter, even though we were not following any cars at the time. It was slightly more acrid, and I could feel it inside my nose and eyes. I would learn later that this was due to the large number of chemical companies like Dow and oil refineries like Amoco who had settled up and down southeast Ohio and used the water from the river in the various processes needed to produce their products. The water they returned to the river contained enough residual chemicals of various sorts to make the river unable to support fish and game or the habitat needed for them to exist. Hence the barren trees and yellow river banks. It wasn't a great first picture for me to see where we would be living. After about 20 minutes, we rounded a bend, and the City of Marietta appeared. Most of it was across an old iron bridge on the east side of the river. Several small paddle wheel riverboats were docked just under the bridge to the south, and many older brick buildings in various states of disrepair lined the river bank. Soon, we turned left and climbed a hill back to the west, winding up to a somewhat flat, sprawling residential area. I was surprised that nearly every house was brick on the outside and not the typical vinyl-sided, modern-looking houses back home. Mostly single-story red and brown brick ranch houses with white trimmed windows, blacktop drives, and one-car garages. The lots were small and not ornately landscaped in any way, making them difficult to discern one from another. We turned right now, just across from a small convenience mart and then up a hill, turning left at the top. The street climbed a hill again, and as it flattened out, Jessie turned into the driveway of the house on the left. It was as described – a brick ranch house with a 1 car attached garage and small blacktop drive. The front yard was small, with a sidewalk in the center from the front step to the street. The backyard sloped steeply away from the house down to a fragile wood-lined creek at the bottom. In the middle of the backyard was a medium-sized "Buckeye" tree. A smattering of "Buckeyes," a small round brown fruit covered with spines similar to a porcupine or sea urchin, was scattered underneath it. I had never seen one before and frankly could have cared less if I had ever seen one again. We went inside the house, and I was pleasantly surprised at how nice it was. It had three bedrooms, two baths, and a finished basement. I asked Jessie how she came up with it and found out the owner was a friend of the station manager and had been trying to sell the house for over a year, but the poor economy in southeast Ohio made it next to impossible. So, he was willing to rent the house to us for $400 per month until he could find a buyer. If we were interested, he might work out a rent-to-own for us. This was the first positive vibe I had since getting off the plane. The kids showed me their room at the end of the hall and wanted me to see the family room downstairs, where they had already spread out some of their toys. They seemed comfortable and at home, which helped calm my anxiety about leaving Minnesota. Maybe the change of scenery would help us come together again and be just what we needed for our family. The kids stayed in the family room and played. Jessie went into the kitchen and started to make something for supper. I unpacked, returned to the living room, and relaxed on the couch. Tomorrow, we would take a tour of the area, and I would grab the local paper and see what job I could land.

Chapter Seventeen:

Coming Undone

The economy of Southeast Ohio and West Virginia during the late 80s and early 90s was extremely depressed. There were basically two industries that dominated the area. One was the chemical producers and oil refiners, and the other was coal mining. The remaining available employment would be either retail or service industry jobs.

As I grabbed the local paper and read classifieds for help, I found an advertisement for chemical engineers, insurance sales associates, grocery store baggers, and shelf stockers. I decided to wait until other choices presented themselves, or if I could find employment via Jessie, I could use her network to hear of possible openings that fit my skill set. I was hoping the local jewelry store or maybe a mall in Parkersburg mall might be looking for a salesperson or manager. In the meantime, I contacted the Ohio National Guard to see if my Wisconsin enlistment could be transferred to Ohio. At least I could attend weekend drills once a month for some kind of income. The only available slot was a Hawk Missile Unit Detachment in McConnelsville, OH. Otherwise, I could re-enlist, start over like a recruit with no rank, and work my way up. I went to McConnelsville and spoke with the unit administrator. The armory in

McConnelsville was small and old. It was a brick building with a few classrooms, two bathrooms, and an old wooden floor gymnasium that acted as the "drill floor" where the company would muster. There were no military vehicles and limited military equipment for training as they had no unit supply section for personnel supplies such as uniforms, field gear, etc. This was because they were a detachment and did not have the security apparatus to protect vehicles, weapons, or gear. That would all be stored with the main unit to which they were attached. Hands-on specialized training for individuals would only take place during their annual training, which is two weeks a year. The only training taking place at McConnelsville was classroom or simulated. It was not something I was used to. After the second time I attended drill, the sergeant responsible for ordering my uniforms said it would be another three months before they arrived. Therefore, I was left in civilian clothes and grouped with recruits who hadn't been to basic training. I had three stripes and had been in for six-plus years. I wasn't going to continue operating in that fashion, so I resigned immediately. My obligation to the United States Army ended that day. I needed to step up my employment search. In the meantime, I was essentially a homemaker. I put Teren on the school bus in the morning as she started kindergarten, and I would take care of Ethan at home. Our day consisted of me getting him up, dressed, fed breakfast, and then doing various activities until Teren came home from school in the afternoon. Ethan and I often read in the morning and then play some indoor game he would choose. Then I would put him in his wagon, and we would go for a walk down to the convenience store to grab a newspaper and treat of some kind. Then, back up the hill to home to play outside. I would feed him lunch, and then we would lay down on my bed to read another book and nap. Invariably, I would fall asleep before he did. Many times, I would awake to see him staring at me, patiently waiting for me to wake up so we could play another game. Luckily, by the time I got out of bed, it was time for the bus to bring Teren home, and his best friend was now there to play with. It took me a few minutes to take a break while the kids played, and I would either watch something on TV, do some housework, or scan the classifieds in the paper to look for new job postings. As this continued for months, I told Jessie I needed a few days without watching the kids so I could go door to door essentially in town and try to find some work. She arranged it so she could be home a couple of afternoons, and I did exactly that. My best hope was the local jewelry store downtown Marietta. It was like Cremer's old downtown store, and I was familiar with many vendors who provided them with inventory. The owner was interested but honestly said that business was not great and they had no opening for another salesperson. He promised that he would give me the first call if that changed. The other stores and businesses were all in the same boat. They were hanging on by a thread and not looking to add employees. As time passed, I began to lose my enthusiasm and quit looking at all. The kids enjoyed having me home and not having to go to any daycare. I could take care of the house inside and out, so at least when Jessie got home, we could spend our time doing something other than housework. I found myself becoming depressed and isolated since I had little adult interaction, no friends, and no connection to the outside world. Jessie had all kinds of energy and was excited about her work. When she came home, I listened to her stories from the office while she made supper, and then she would spend time with the kids before making her nightly brandy and finding her spot on the sofa downstairs to watch her shows. We were drifting apart, and she appeared to have no interest in what I thought or felt. After nearly a year of this, my depression was starting to overwhelm me. It made me moody and anxious. I realized it was time for Jessie and me to discuss what was happening and how I felt. I wasn't sure I could keep being a house husband and was genuinely concerned that I had been out of the workforce so long that I could never find a job again.

One night, after the kids were in bed, I called down to the family room and asked Jessie to come upstairs that I needed to talk to her. She grudgingly came up, and I asked her to come to the bedroom to talk without the kids hearing, just in case they were not sleeping yet. I began by telling her about my job concerns and how I was worried about not being employed for so long. She understood but didn't seem to care. I also told her that I was struggling with feeling very lonely and that I needed some emotional support from her. I told her that, on occasion, I was so down that I started crying because I didn't feel like she had any feelings for me anymore. She looked at me almost disgustedly and said, "Oh, Jesus Christ, Jay! Grow up. Nobody cares about your feelings." In that instant, I exploded. I grabbed her, threw her on the bed, climbed on top of her with my knees pinning down her arms, and placed both my hands around her throat. I screamed at the top of my lungs, "You don't have to fucking love me, but God Dammit, you are going to respect me," and I started squeezing her throat. Her eyes began to bulge, her face turned red, and no sound came out of her wide-open mouth. Just then, there was a knock on the bedroom door. Teren had heard me scream, and she asked through the door, "Are you okay, Daddy?" It brought me back to reality, and I released my grip and got off Jessie. I spoke through the door to Teren, "Yes, sweetheart, I'm okay. You can go back to bed, and I will be there in a minute." I heard her little footsteps back down the hall. By that time, Jessie had gotten off the bed. She stood there coughing as she tried to catch her breath. She looked at me in shock. The reality of what just happened hit me, and I nearly collapsed. I foolishly told her I was sorry and did not mean to do that. I asked if she was okay. I could see red fingerprints on her neck. I left the room and went down the hall to the kid's room. I sat on the bed next to Teren and told her I was okay and that she should just go to sleep. She closed her eyes and went to sleep. Tears filled my eyes while I looked at my beautiful children. I sat by her, quietly weeping. Jessie went into the bathroom to check on herself in the mirror. After a few minutes, I left the kids' room and returned to Jessie. I told her I was sorry again, loved her, and thought it was time to leave. I went downstairs to the family room, lay on the couch, and stared into the darkness, trying to understand what I had done and would do now. Jessie stayed upstairs and in the bedroom. We slept apart that night for the first time in our marriage. The next day was a Saturday, so Jessie didn't have to work. She came downstairs in the morning before the kids woke up and said we needed to talk. I said that is what I wanted to do last night before I lost it. She said she had no idea that I was feeling so bad. She told me I scared her, but she was feeling okay, and the marks on her neck were already gone. I assured her that I would never do something like that again. I didn't know that her dismissal of my feelings would make me react that way. I had only ever had that switch flipped before, which was back in college when I went after Jim Bradford. I told her that not having a job, no friends, and no adult conversation all just kept building up inside me, and I could not take it anymore. I said I thought the best thing was to spend some time away from her and the kids to sort out my feelings and give her a chance to decide if we would stay married. Until we could figure out how that was going to happen, I promised that I would not ask anything of her, and she didn't need to worry about another incident of that kind again. We would not alert the kids to anything and act like normal. Jessie was good with that. For the next few weeks, Jessie seemed closer to me than she had been in a long time for some strange reason. Maybe it was an act. Maybe she was realizing that I was seriously considering leaving, and our relationship for nearly ten years was in jeopardy. I don't know. I had lost myself somewhere over the last ten years. It felt like everything I had tried failed. Were the sacrifices I had made for my family also going to be wasted? My dad's voice bounced around in my mind like a superball that could never come to rest and I could never get a hold of. It would keep telling me that I was an educated idiot. That I wasn't tough enough to make it, that I was still the baby of the family, tugging on my mother's apron strings. I had gotten my ass beaten many times as a kid. Often having raised red welts that burned to the touch so I couldn't sit down. Who was he to tell me I was soft and had nothing to cry about? My very being was coming apart like a snowman in the spring sunlight. All that remains to prove he existed are a hat, a scarf, a few buttons, and a partially chewed carrot, all lying in disarray on the ground. How many winters could I come back to life?

Chapter Eighteen:

Blessed Friends

I spent the next few weeks trying to figure out where I would go and what I would do. The only option I could think of was to call my folks and see if they would be willing to have me stay there until I could re-establish myself. I dreaded making that phone call, but I had no other choice. Then, out of the blue, I got a call from Bob Church, the manager at Lasker's in Rochester. He was calling to see what I was doing and to make me aware of an opportunity he thought I would be interested in. Charles Lasker was offered the chance to purchase a competing jewelry store in Rochester, whose owner was retiring. Charles thought he would buy it and run a going-out-of-business sale to see if he could make a quick profit and liquidate some of his inventory from the three stores he owned. Charles and Bob agreed I would be an excellent choice to run the operation for him. So Bob was asked to call me and find out if I would be interested and, if so, what it would take for me to take the job. I told him that I was interested but would have to figure out how to get there and where I would live before I could give him an answer. I said I would call him back in a couple of days. When Jessie got home, I told her of the call and discussed whether we wanted this.

She would be left with kids alone in Ohio, and I would be in Minnesota alone, but I would send money back to her as needed. The job could last up to 6 months, which should give us enough time to decide where our marriage stood. She was in favor, and we would tell the kids together, hoping they would be alright. She would have to secure some daycare we both felt comfortable with before I could go. I got a call from a good friend named Sandy Johnson, whom I had worked with at Lasker's. Bob had told the sales staff about what Charles was planning to do and that he was trying to get me back to do it. Sandy talked to her husband Jerry in her sweet and giving way and thought they could help me. So she and her husband Jerry offered to let me stay in their basement bedroom until I found my own place if I took the job. They lived in Zumbrota, Minnesota, just 20 miles north of Rochester on Hwy 52. She didn't ask for any rent but agreed with my insistence to take $100 monthly to cover the added expense of utilities and food. The other nice thing was that I could ride to work with Sandy as the store hours were the same, so I didn't need a vehicle immediately. I called my folks and told them I had an opportunity for some work in Rochester and asked if they would be willing to get me and take me to a friend's house in Zumbrota, MN, to stay while I worked at the store. I didn't tell them anything about my marriage issues but that this was just a financial decision and that I couldn't afford to fly home. It would also allow them to see the kids since they hadn't seen them for nearly a year. They were okay with that; I just needed to let them know when. So I called Bob Church back and told him I would take the job for $500.00 per week plus a $1500.00 bonus to help me get settled somewhere once I got going. Bob gave Charles my terms, and Charles said yes. I was unhappy to leave, but I needed to do something. My folks came down the next week and stayed for a few days. Jessie acted as though we were all doing wonderful and showed off her office at the station in Parkersburg. The day came to leave, so I put my bags in the car trunk and then hugged my kids, telling them I would see them again in just a few months. I told them to be good and listen to Mommy, and I would call every couple of days to talk with them. Thankfully, they were young enough not to be distraught and waved feverishly to me as the car pulled away. I sat in the backseat, waving just as hard back at them and trying to smile. As we got out of sight, my eyes welled with tears, not really knowing when I would see my kids again. I sat very silently, trying not to talk or sniffle loud enough to have my mom or dad hear. I was dying inside. I knew I would be okay where I was going and what I would be doing, but I was very unsure what Jessie would do and how it might affect my kids. Ethan and I had gotten so close, and he was used to our daily activities and his wagon ride. I was afraid nobody else, including his mother, would take that. kind of time with him. It was a long ride back to Black River Falls, and when we got home, I settled back into my old bedroom for the night. I called Jessie and the kids and told them we got home all right and that I missed them. The next day, I called Sandy in Zumbrota and arranged a time for me to come over and move in. She and Jerry were inviting and willing to make it easy for me. So, on the next Saturday, my dad would drive me over. Mom stayed home. Dad always liked to take road trips and see new places and usually stopped at houses along the way that might have a car for sale in the yard. That was an Eddy tradition. That was also why my mother stayed home because a trip that should have taken a couple of hours could always turn into three or four hours while my dad visited with the would-be sellers about everything under the sun. My mother would have to wait in the car for the visit to end. We arrived at Sandy's house and parked in the driveway in front of the two-car detached garage at the back of the house. Sandy had a big square white two-story house on the corner lot. I walked up to the door and knocked to let them know I arrived. Sandy and Jerry both came out to welcome me and meet my dad. We visited for a while, and Sandy offered my dad to come in and have a cup of coffee if he wished. My dad declined and decided he better get back home. He said goodbye and left without any fanfare.

Jerry helped me bring my luggage into the house through the back door. Immediately inside the door was a small round wooden dining room table with four wooden chairs, each having a red seat cushion. This was an attached nook to the kitchen, which opened to the left. It was a long, wide hallway kind of kitchen with dark oak cabinets on the walls and the counters of a lighter Formica wood grain. The floors were covered with a kind of red patterned flat pile carpet. Jerry led the way to the end of the kitchen, and the doorway to the basement was on the far wall. They left it open all the time for their cat to be able to go down and get to the litter box, and it was easier for Sandy to get down when carrying the clothes basket to the washer and dryer that were down there also. Jerry turned on the light, and we walked down the stairs to reveal one larger room with a pull-out sofa bed already made up for me. To the right was the bathroom and the laundry room. There was no closet but a small three-door chest of drawers and a portable clothes rack for hanging clothes. The floor did have a brown sculptured carpet that made it warmer, softer, and muffled noise. Jerry had also brought down a portable black and white TV that he hooked up to his antenna so I could watch local TV on my own. I thanked him for everything, and he said no problem. He also hoped I didn't have any problems with cat allergies, as he suspected the cat would be down to visit me from time to time. He was an orange tiger cat, and Jerry warned me that he was fond of jumping on beds at night to sleep. I wasn't overly concerned. Jerry then left me to get settled and said Sandy would be hollering down when supper would be ready, and I could come up and join them. It wasn't long before Sandy stood at the top of the stairs and told me it was time to eat. I went upstairs, and they showed me into the formal dining room off the living room. The two rooms were painted light blue and had a soft blue shag carpet. The dining room table was a larger dark wood square table. Jerry sat on one farthest from the kitchen, and Sandy sat on the other, closest to the kitchen. On one side of the table sat their two girls—Amber and Brittany.

Amber was 8, and Brittany was 6. They were both pretty little girls favoring their mother and making me think the three of them would have made a set of nesting dolls. Sandy and Jerry were devout Catholics, and saying grace at mealtime was expected. After grace, we had a nice meal and pleasant visit, talking about all kinds of things like working together at Laskers, my family, Amber and Brittany's school etc. I was impressed with the girl's manners. They said please and thank you, waited to speak until someone else was finished, and then asked to be excused when they finished eating. Mom and Dad were in charge and had spent time with these children, which developed a healthy, happy relationship. Jerry and Sandy had the same kind of relationship with each other. After supper, I offered to do the dishes, but Sandy said she and Amber would take care of that. So Jerry invited me into the living room to watch TV and talk about various topics as they came to mind. Jerry and Sandy were from Mosinee, Wisconsin, so the Packers were their football team. Jerry was a real conservative and proud to say he was a state delegate to the Republican convention. Sandy just deferred to Jerry when it came to politics, as she was not as vocal in that arena and spent most evenings with the girls doing homework. By 9:00 pm, the girls said good night and went upstairs to bed in an orderly fashion. I decided that was my cue to excuse myself so that Jerry and Sandy could have time together without my presence. That would be our routine. I went downstairs and crawled into bed with the TV playing at a low level. After the news, I turned it off and went to sleep. Sometime in the middle of the night, I could feel the cat jump onto the bed and walk around investigating this new visitor to his territory. If I stayed still, he would find a spot and lay down, but if I moved, he would jump off and quickly dash back up the stairs to safety.

The next morning, I could hear the family wake up and move about above me. I looked at the clock and realized it was time to get up and ready for work. Sandy was friendly enough to call down and see if I was awake and invite me for breakfast. I acknowledged that I had arisen but passed on the breakfast. I tried as often as I could not to interfere with their routines. Once Jerry and the girls had left, Sandy told me it was time to go, and I came upstairs to head to work. Zumbrota was about a ½ hour trip to Rochester. It was nice to have a ride to work and someone to visit, both going and coming home again. Sometimes, Sandy would ask me to drive the car so she could get a few minutes of rest. Sandy had been in a car accident several years before, and the result was a painful back injury and migraine headaches that showed up unannounced from time to time. So, I was more than happy to give her a break from driving and talking so she could work her way through the pain and prepare for the workday. By Friday of the first week, I was settled in my job and living conditions. In a rather ironic twist, I got a call from Jessie saying that the jewelry store in Marietta called and had an opening. They were hoping I would be interested. I called them from Minnesota and appreciated their interest, but I had already committed to this job in Rochester and couldn't leave at this point. They understood, and I told them I would call them once this was over and I was back in Marietta. I thought—only if they had called two weeks earlier.

Life at Sandy and Jerry's was good. I missed my wife and children, but between work and some interactions with the world again, I started to feel myself healing and coming out of my depression. I was able to send money home and have enough for me to take care of my needs. After two months, I got a rather unexpected phone call. Jessie called to say she was unhappy at her job and that she and the kids would move back to Rochester. She had contacted someone at KROC radio in Rochester, and there was an advertising sales position available that she was going to take. As they return to Rochester, I'll explore potential homes for us. I was so happy to see my children again and felt that Jessie and I could reconnect as a couple. I told Jerry and Sandy the news, and they were very happy for me. They said they enjoyed having me as a guest and that the girls considered me their uncle.

I could never repay the kindness and generosity that they had shown to me. Some three years later, Jerry would die of a massive heart attack while raking in the front yard. Amber found him lying there and tried CPR to no avail. Tests would show he had an undiagnosed enlarged heart, and it was likely the cause. Two years after Jerry's death, Sandy would suffer a stroke and fight hard to be able to return to a normal life again. My life would also be very different by then. In the meantime, Jessie and the kids were coming home. I had every reason to believe our future was bright. I didn't realize how far from shore we were.

Chapter Nineteen:

All That Glitters

The store Charles had purchased was Suskovic's Jewelry, located on the first floor of the Holiday Inn downtown Rochester on Broadway Street. It was a mom-and-pop store as the couple had run it for years. Mr. Suskovic had passed away, and Mrs. Suskovic was at an age where she couldn't run a store independently. She also really had no desire either, having lost her lifelong love and business partner. I have no idea what Charles paid for it, but I suspect it wasn't much. Charles always believed that you don't make money when you sell something but when you buy it. Buy low and sell high.

We reviewed the inventory, and the store was obviously tired and, in many cases, fashionably obsolete. My job was to clean it up, rearrange it, price it high enough to give a considerable discount, and still make money. Most of all, Charles would say, "Don't fall in love with the merchandise. Get this shit sold." So that was my challenge. Charles also brought in a couple of carloads of "the dogs" he had purchased through the 40-plus years in business in Eau Claire and his other Rochester store. I was on my own as far as running the store was concerned. I had no other full-time employees and just one part-time person. That turned out to be Bob Church's daughter, Molly, who would come down after school in the afternoons. That gave me a break to eat lunch and help put everything away in the safe at closing time. Molly was a sweet, intelligent, pretty girl who giggled a lot while I tried to teach her about selling jewelry. She also had a little rebellious side that many teens do and occasionally would share her displeasure with her parents about happenings in her life. I listened like an older brother promising not to share secrets with her dad or anyone else.

After about a month or so, Bob told me he was going to be sending me another full-time employee whom he wanted me to train in all the aspects of the jewelry business, from sales to display, purchasing, and everything I knew about every type of jewelry, gold, watches, etc. That person was Hans Soukup. Bob brought Hans to Suskovic's and introduced him to me. He said Hans was going to be working full-time. I welcomed Hans, and we started getting to know each other immediately and the task at hand. Hans had just graduated from Luther College in Iowa with a degree in business management. He was about 6 feet tall and 190 lbs. Strong build with a very youthful face. I learned he played quarterback for the Luther College football team. I made him aware that my best friend had played football there as well, which led to us having conversations about things other than jewelry. Hans had a quick wit and a pleasant sense of humor. He reminded me of my college roommates, making coming to work more enjoyable. We worked hard together and enjoyed making each other laugh while working. Hans would become a good friend of mine and an important assistant for me to depend on to get through the sale. I also learned that Hans' father, a friend of Bob's, facilitated his hiring in Rochester through their connection.

As the sale progressed, we had become busier and busier and would need to hire more help. Bob decided we would use a temporary agency in Rochester to get that help. It worked well, and I essentially was the coach, with Hans as my assistant coach, and we trained and developed a very productive sales staff. We went from doing hundreds of dollars of business a day to thousands. Charles enjoyed the process and even bought more jewelry to keep the trough full. Bob wasn't quite as happy because we were taking some of his customers from Lasker's. The public had no idea we were connected in any way, and it was one of our biggest rules not to let anyone know that. Every once in a while, I would call Bob, ask for some items I knew he had in his stock, and see if he was willing to part with them so we could sell them at Suskovic's. Work couldn't be going any better, making it easier for me to concentrate on finding a place to live as Jessie and the kids were on the way.

We never had enough money to buy a house. It was a function of not being good at saving, not making much money, having two kids, high-interest rates, and moving so many times we couldn't establish ourselves anywhere. So, our only housing choice would be to rent like always. I found a decent two-bedroom apartment in Summit Square in Rochester. It was close to a big park and a short walk to Gage Elementary School, so the kids didn't have to ride a bus. We were on the second floor, just down from the laundry room. We were on the south side of the building, so we had a nice amount of sunshine and a good view of the parking lot and the park. The kids and Jessie approved, and we got moved in. I reconnected with the kids right away, and they were excited at the idea of being able to walk to the park and school. The downside of renting is that you don't have a lot of storage or a garage. The small store room we did have was filled rather quickly. We bought a bike for the kids to ride and locked it outside on the bike rack. Ethan was just learning to ride a bike, which didn't take long. He also wanted to see how fast he could go like all small boys. Unfortunately, he wasn't the best at stopping. He twice drove into the glass entry door to the building, shattering the glass. They didn't charge us for the repair the first time, but it cost $150.00 the second time. At least he didn't get hurt or hit anyone else. Jessie seemed happy to be home, and without any conversations about our relationship, it felt like we were coming back together again. She even would stop by the store during the day to see how the sales were going, and we would have lunch together—something we had never done in the over ten years of marriage. I was encouraged and felt like we survived a rough patch, but the time apart taught us how we needed each other. It also put us back into the routine of going down to the farm like we had in the past. Not much had changed except that Jessie's siblings had gotten older and were starting their own families. We were no longer needed as the safe house or foster home for the kids seeking refuge from the drunken antics of their father. Jessie still had her car, and I was able to scratch up enough to buy a vehicle for me. It was a 4-door Plymouth Horizon with a hatchback. It had 60 plus thousand miles but was in good shape and good on gas with a tiny 4 - 4-cylinder engine. It was gold in color, so I nicknamed it Golde, like the character from Fiddler on the Roof. It was a good runner and easy to park downtown, which was nice. We were enjoying life for the first time in a while. The kids met Hans, and they thought of him like an uncle. He would wrestle around with Ethan and play games with them whenever he came over to visit. Jessie wasn't quite as enamored with him as she thought he was egotistical and kind of a smart ass because he would poke fun at everyone. She never could laugh at herself about anything. She was the oldest child in her family, so she was used to giving orders to everyone. I never let it bother me, but Hans would pick up on that and give her some grief about being so bossy.

It was the spring of 1992, and we would be celebrating our 11th marriage anniversary in March. We had been together for almost 13 years. It was difficult at times, but despite those troubles and the fact that I hadn't accomplished what I wanted professionally, I was happy that my family was back together. I should have known better.

"Why do you not even know what will happen tomorrow? What is your life? You are a mist that appears for a little while and then vanishes." James 4:14

Chapter Twenty:

Adrift

By the summer, things at Suskovic's were going to be coming to an end. In a strange twist of fate, another jeweler in Rochester wanted to retire, and it just so happened that Charles decided to buy that store as well. It was Cecil Jewelers, just a half a block from Lasker's downtown. Charles was thrilled with the results of the Suskovic liquidation, as we had done over half a million in sales. So, the plan was to close the Suskovic store, move to Cecil's, and continue the liquidation game until sometime in November. That was good news for me and Hans as we could continue working together, and I was especially happy to stay employed for the foreseeable future. I was making decent money, and Charles came through with some additional bonuses for us both for doing a great job at Suskovic's.

Our home life was busy but good for the most part. Then, one night, something happened that would change our routine. Teren would often have trouble going to sleep at night, and she would ask if she could sit with me on the couch until she fell asleep, and I would put her in bed. As usual, she fell asleep that night, and I lifted her off the couch and carried her to her bed. As I bent over to lay her down as softly as possible,

Jay Eddy

something popped in my back. I felt a sudden, very sharp, burning pain, and I was unable to stand upright. I had never experienced pain like that before, and I was very concerned. I crawled into my bedroom and up into the bed. I awoke Jessie and said that I had hurt my back and wasn't sure what to do. She grabbed me some Tylenol, and I lay as quietly as I could, trying not to move. The burning had subsided by morning, but the pain was still there. As I tried to get out of bed, my back went into full spasm, dropping me back onto the bed again. I told Jessie that I thought I had a serious injury and that I needed to go to the doctor. We were able to get an appointment at Mayo later that day, so I struggled to get into the car and the clinic.

X-rays didn't show any disc damage, but the doctor's exam led him to diagnose a back sprain of the L-1 vertebrae facet joint, which means basically that I tore the ligament on that vertebrae similar to what you would do to a knee or an ankle. It was a serious soft tissue injury that had no cure. They didn't recommend any kind of surgery at that time because of the dangers associated with nerve damage and back surgery. So, he prescribed painkillers and muscle relaxers to help with spasms and then gave me a back brace that I was to wear for the next six months to a year. He said that I might seek some relief from chiropractic treatments and that after six weeks, I should have some relief and start physical therapy to strengthen the muscles and improve healing.

I was angry and frustrated that I would have to curtail my activities. It also made me quite anxious as I kept getting back spasms with the simplest of movements or bending. I couldn't even lift a laundry basket of clothes. I no longer could play on the floor with the kids and give them horseback rides on all fours. It made everything I did more difficult. It also added another level of tension to my relationship with Jessie. She was now going to have to do many of the things that I had been doing, like the housework, taking the kids to the park etc. She was less than understanding and gave me the impression that she thought I was faking the pain or that I should be able to get through it easier. What kind of man was I? I did everything the doctors told me, but this injury would stay with me for the rest of my life. Although the initial injury has

166

healed, it has left behind scar tissue, making areas such as a trick knee or ankle prone to re-injury. Many times, over the years, I'd suffer back spasms from overactivity as the muscles surrounding that joint tightened to protect it from possible injury. It took the fun out of a lot of my life and caused me some psychological pain as well. I felt less than whole, weak, and ashamed of being unable to do things others could. It's not a visible injury, so people often don't relate or understand unless they have experienced the agony of back spasms. They are debilitating. I learned to live with them and eventually was able to go without a brace for extended periods unless I had a massive relapse.

Later that fall, Jessie decided that our life was dull, and all we did was work and stay home. I told her that I wished it could be different, but we didn't have the money to do a lot of extra things, and physically, I was still trying to recover from my back issue. She decided to join, of all things, a bowling league with her sister Jordie. It gave her a chance to get out of the house one night a week for something other than a work event and a reason to have a few or more drinks. I would have rather had her find something to do with the kids for one night a week, but she didn't think much of that idea. As the weeks went by, she would come home later and later from her bowling night. I learned from her other sister, Julie, that her bowling league was for mixed couples.

Something Jessie forgot to tell me when she started. I asked her about it, and she wondered what difference it made. I told her it made a difference to me, and I'm sure if I had done something similar, she wouldn't be happy about it. Nevertheless, she was unmoved and made it clear that it was her business and not mine. There was a sense of defiance with a hint of deception in her tone. It made me uneasy and gave me the impression that there was more to this than meets the eye. Strangely, from that night on, I would start having a recurring dream where she would laugh at me behind my back, or when I approached her in some circumstance, she pretended not to know me.

Even though it was a dream, I started having some anxiety and paranoia about the future. I didn't say anything to anyone about how I was feeling and just concentrated on work. By the end of October, the sale at Cecil's was going full swing with great success. Charles came in one day and told us that by State Law in Minnesota, we could no longer run the sale for another 30 days, so we would close on the day before Thanksgiving in November. I spoke with him about continuing to work at Lasker's after the closing. He told me it was up to Bob to decide if he needed help for the Christmas season. I then spoke with Bob, and he said that he had one opening for a salesperson for Christmas, and he had already arranged for Hans to fill it. He was sorry, but I would be let go after the sale and be unemployed then. I understood, but it hurt to think that after all the years I worked for Lasker's and the effort I put into the liquidations, I would be on the outside. It couldn't have come at a worse time in my life. I fought hard to overcome the feelings of depression, anger, and even resentment toward Hans for taking what I thought should have been my job. He didn't have anything to do with the decision-making. I felt like I had been used by people I had worked for and befriended. I was good enough to do all the hard work and make everyone happy, but not considered part of the family.

My feelings were hurt, and I was very anxious about how I would support my family when Thanksgiving came. I went home and told Jessie about what would happen and that I would be out of work come Thanksgiving. She offered no condolences or words of comfort. She was detached and almost clinical in her response. No tears, no sadness, no compassion for what I was going through, but only a kind of annoyance that she would have to limit her lifestyle because of my failure. The weight of the future was upon me like a dive belt that made it easier to sink and stay underwater. I also felt a real separation from Jessie. There was a strange, cold emptiness in her eyes, and she would recoil as if being burned if I touched her. The only comfort and compassion I felt was with my children. I held them tighter and absorbed as much of their love as I could to help renew me. I kept telling myself that as long as they were ok, nothing else mattered, and I could make it through. The truth of this statement was about to be tested.

Surviving Myself

The final day of the sale arrived. It was the Wednesday before Thanksgiving. We had terrific sales, and I was thrilled with what we had done. I felt pretty close to the people I was working with. It was a bittersweet goodbye to all, especially Hans, who, in some sense, felt like my younger brother. We agreed to stay in touch, and he thanked me profusely for everything I taught him and the experience we shared. He was sorry about how it worked out with him being able to stay working and me being let go. I told him to do his best and remember everything I taught him, and he would succeed. As it turned out, he would move to Eau Claire to work for Charles in his new store next to the mall. Hans would help manage and be the buyer. He is still there to this day, and I have stopped to see him a number of times over the years. He always reminisces about the old days.

I went home after work, and because it was bowling night, I would make supper and then take care of the kids for the evening. I put the kids to bed and stayed up to watch the news. I was expecting Jessie to be home soon, so I stayed awake, hoping to share the "last day" events. Midnight came and went, and still no Jessie. My mind started playing out various scenarios of what was going on. Maybe she had car trouble, or maybe she had to give Jordie a ride home. Maybe they just got partying a little and lost track of time. Maybe something was going on that shouldn't be. My feelings were all over the place. I went from concern to anger the longer I had to wait. I tried to lie down and go to sleep, but my adrenaline was high, and I just couldn't relax enough to go to sleep. I lay on the bed and kept checking the alarm clock. The red numbers glowed with 1:00 and no Jessie. I started practicing what I was going to say when she arrived. I was mad; she better know I would not accept her coming home this late again. Every minute that passed seemed like an hour. As my tension grew, I could feel my back tighten as well. I did some deep breathing, trying to calm myself to avoid some emotional stress that might lead to my back spasming. At about 2:00 AM, I heard the door open, and Jessie shuffle in. She came in quietly so as not to wake the kids, but she was surprised to find me still awake as I turned the lamp on in the bedroom. I could tell she had been drinking plenty. I asked her where she was and what she had been doing until 2:00 in the morning. I know she wasn't bowling until that hour. I felt like a parent interrogating an unruly teenager. She told me point blank that she went out after bowling with Jordie and the guys on the team. Then she said, "I don't know how to say this, so I will just come out and say it. I want a divorce. I have hired an attorney, and I would like you to be out of the house by New Year, or I will take the kids and leave." There was no emotion in her voice. She couldn't look me in the eyes, and she went through her routine to go to bed. I stood in stunned silence. In one instance, I loved and hated her at the same time. I tried to speak quietly so the kids didn't hear. I asked her, "How am I supposed to find another place to live? I lost my job today and have no income, or did you forget?" And then, as if this was some trivial issue, she said, "I don't know, but we will have to talk about it tomorrow." I need to sleep because we have to go to the farm tomorrow for Thanksgiving, and Mom wants me to bring some pies." She crawled into bed, grabbed the covers, and rolled into a ball facing away from my side of the bed.

I left the room and headed to the living room. I lay on the couch staring into the darkness with tears streaming down my face. The reality of what was happening felt like being told I had a terminal incurable disease. There was no sleep for me that night. It was all I could do to breathe. My hands were shaking, and all my nerves were firing simultaneously. Soon, I heard the alarm in the bedroom, and shortly after, Jessie came out of the bedroom and headed to the kitchen.

I entered the kitchen and initiated a conversation. "What happened?" I inquired. In response, she declared her desire for a divorce. She claimed that there was nothing specific and that she realized she didn't love me anymore and wanted her freedom. I asked her if she knew what that would do to the kids and if she was sure about it. She said she had been thinking about it for a long time and finally had the courage to say it last night. I said I didn't really understand. Then I asked her how we would tell the kids and when this was supposed to happen. She wanted me to agree that we would wait until after Christmas to tell everyone in our families and the kids. I wasn't sure I could do that. I also told her

I needed to talk to someone about my rights. She then reminded me that she already retained an attorney, and he said to her that because I was unemployed and didn't have my own place to live, the court would unlikely award me custody. That pissed me off, and I said, "Well, isn't that fucking convenient." Then I told her that I could pretend for the sake of the kids and the family, but I was going to call a few attorneys and find out for myself. She looked at me, kind of surprised and miffed. "Whatever," she snipped.

By then, the kids had arisen and came into the kitchen looking for breakfast. Our conversation stopped, and we attended to their needs. I left the kitchen, showered, and got ready for our "Happy Thanksgiving" at the farm. It was tough for me to watch Jessie pretend that nothing was happening and laugh and smile with her family, knowing fully well that this would be the last time we would celebrate this the same way. Over the next month, we would have numerous discussions about the divorce.

I had called some attorneys; of course, they needed a retainer that I couldn't afford. Jessie had cleverly spent all our extra money on getting her attorney. I pleaded with her several times to avoid going through with it. She just couldn't understand how I was unable to accept the decision. I told her I loved her and the kids more than anything in the world. Her mind was made up. So, I called her attorney and asked if he could handle the entire divorce and explained my position regarding the kids and support. He was willing to work directly with me, and I made him aware that I would represent myself if need be, and I didn't have any money to pay him for any work. He understood and explained that he could write the divorce decree with the terms that Jessie and I agreed with, but the court may order something different. Frankly, I didn't want my kids to have to move again or take things away from them. I was more concerned about the emotional impact.

My emotional state was in constant flux, going from deep hurt to despair, to anger, to complete emptiness. Somehow, we got to and through Christmas, and the time came to tell the kids and for me to find another place to live. Jessie took the lead, telling the kids she and

I would divorce. She tried to explain that I would still be their dad but live somewhere else. I tried like hell to keep from crying as she spoke the words out loud. The kids weren't sure what it meant, but they could see that I was hurting, and it must be bad if Daddy was crying. Through the sobs, I did my best to tell them that it was going to be alright. Then, to fix the problem, Ethan said, "Dad, just tell Mom you're sorry, and everything will be okay." I said, "I can't, buddy; I didn't do anything to be sorry for, and even if I said it, Mommy still wants me to leave." He started to cry and climbed up on his mother's lap and looked at her, wondering why. She held him tight, and for the first time, I saw her with a tear in her eye. We all just sat silently for a few minutes. Some pain is so bad that it's impossible to speak.

Chapter Twenty One:

Breaking Point

My unemployment compensation has been set at $280.00 per week. It was just over half of what I was making before. So, Jessie and I started searching for the cheapest place for me to live in Rochester. We hoped to find something near the elementary school so the kids could walk to my place after school just like they were used to walking home. We found a 1-bedroom efficiency in the Winchester Apartment complex. The apartment features a living room, a combined dining room and kitchen, a bathroom, and one bedroom.

Rochester was in the middle of an economic and housing boom in the early 90s. This fueled the rental market, so trying to find something cheap was next to impossible. It was going to cost me $400.00 per month. I did get a break on the security deposit and only had to put up $250.00 instead of the $400.00. Having that settled, it was time to decide what I would be taking from the old place to live. I ended up with two chairs, a 19-inch TV, one end table, one lamp, a single bed mattress with no frame, three glasses, three plates, three sets of silverware, three towels, 1 set of sheets, a comforter that we had been given for a wedding present, my clothes, and my car. That was everything I would own from twelve years of marriage. I had very little room for much more than that anyway, and my apartment was on the second floor, so moving in was easier with less to carry. The kids liked the place and were excited about camping out on the bedroom floor when they would stay with me.

The first week, I tried to occupy my mind with finding work and not thinking about Jessie. Nights were tough, and I often would start crying when I laid down to sleep. I stayed up later and later to avoid going to bed. I was having trouble eating as well. I guess the emotional strain took away my desire to eat. Then, one night, Jessie's sister Jordie called me for some reason. She was always close to me, and she even came and lived with us during a rough period in her teen years when she had gotten pregnant out of wedlock. Her father was angry and verbally abusive, which made it difficult for her to be home. We took her in for a summer until the storm at home died. Jordie wanted me to know how sorry she was for what had happened and that she would miss me. She also wanted me to know that Jessie had met someone else while they had been bowling. She wanted me to know that she had nothing to do with the relationship. I told her that I felt there was someone else and that Jessie was hiding something from me. I asked if she knew the guy. She said yes. His name was John, and he worked at IBM. He was recently divorced, and according to Jordie, she thought he was a very nice guy. He had a lot of money, a house, an RV, a boat, and all kinds of adult toys. He had two children, one boy who was high school age and a daughter who was the same age as Teren. I told Jordie I appreciated her being honest and held no anger at her for what happened with Jessie and me. We said goodbye, and I hung up the phone.

The news of Jessie's affair only served to ramp up my anger, anxiety, shame, and feelings of worthlessness. I wanted very much to call Jessie right up and start cussing her out for being so damned dishonest and unfaithful. It made every conversation with her from that point forward extremely difficult. I wanted her to know that I thought she was a "God Damned liar." I wanted her to feel as badly as I did or worse. At the same time, I was falling apart, living with the reality that the person I loved and trusted most had betrayed me in the worst way. One night, after the kids had called me to tell me about the day we visited, I told them goodnight and put mommy on the phone. Jessie got on, and I told her Jordie told me the truth. I told her that I believed that John was likely not the first. After cussing and swearing and crying and everything else, I told her thanks for taking away everything that ever mattered to me in my life. She said something to the effect that I would have to learn to get on with life. I told her that, at this point, I wasn't sure if I wanted to get on with this life, and I hung up the phone. What a fool I had been. How could I have ever fallen in love with someone like her? Yet, if she had said she loved me and was sorry, I would have gone back. I went to the bedroom and lay on the bed with a more energetic crying episode than usual. Then a knock came to my door. I never had anyone knock on my door, and I was dumbfounded by who it could be. I dried my eyes, took a deep breath to compose myself, and then went to answer the door. I was expecting that one of my neighbors would ask me to keep it down as maybe I had been too loud. Instead, it was a police officer from the city of Rochester. He identified himself and asked if he could step inside. I let him in, not knowing why he would be coming to see me. He said that a call had come from Jessie Eddy, and she was concerned that I may be considering suicide. He was there to check on me. I had no idea what to say. I was so pissed at her for calling the cops, but I hid that from him. He asked me a few questions about our relationship and how I felt about what was happening. Then the phone rang, and it was my brother Randy. He was calling to check on me as Jessie had called him. What was she doing? I was in a state of unbelief. I told him that she was crazy and that we had a fight on the phone, and now I had the Rochester police in my apartment. He was trying to reassure me and was concerned based on what Jessie had told him. I tried to make a few jokes about her and what was happening and that when I settled down, I would call him back and please don't tell Mom or Dad about this. I have no idea how I looked, but the officer then asked if I would be willing to go with him to St. Mary's Hospital for a quick evaluation of my mental state. There was no pressure, and he said they take people there daily to ensure they are okay. He would give me a ride there and back when it was over. He had a friendly and caring tone and did his best to convince me that it was the right thing to do. So, I agreed to go with him. He told me to sit in the front seat with him, and we talked while we drove to the hospital. He said he had seen several of these situations before and understood what I was going through. He told me not to feel bad about going with him and that after talking to the counselor, he was sure I would feel better. We arrived, and he escorted me into the building. He stopped and talked to the nurse behind the desk, and I sat in the waiting area. He came over and told me that they would call, and he would give me a ride back home when I was ready. I thanked him, and he left. Soon, another nurse came and took me to a room, letting me know that the doctor would be in to see me shortly. Within a few minutes, a female doctor entered the room. She introduced herself and told me she was a psychologist with Mayo and worked at St. Mary's in the mental health department. She was calm and reassuring, and we simply talked about what I was feeling and going through for about an hour. She helped me realize that these highly charged emotional life events are difficult for most people to handle. It would be a good thing if I had someone to talk to. She also felt like I needed some distance from the source of my anxiety and feelings. In other words, getting away from Jessie and limiting my interactions with her could help me start dealing with the loss. She equated it to someone dying, and the feelings are very much the same. The trouble with divorce is that the person we are grieving about losing isn't actually gone, so we try, often in vain, to hang onto the relationship. It gave me plenty to think about, and then she gave me her card and told me to call if I needed to follow up in the future.

I felt better and thanked her very much just for listening and understanding. As promised, they called the policeman who brought me, and he gave me a ride home again. That night, I went straight to bed, contemplating a move back to Black River as a much-needed escape from Jessie. It would mean being farther away from my kids, but at this point, I struggled to be the dad I had been when we were all together anyway. I needed to heal somehow. Exhaustion took over, and I fell asleep without realizing it.

Chapter Twenty Two:

To Be Or Not To Be

O ur divorce hearing was scheduled for March 3, 1993. I had given Jessie virtually all our personal property of any value. She also took our new car, a 1992 Chrysler New Yorker, and the payments for it. I was able to get visitation with the kids anytime I wanted with her getting full-time placement. The court would order that they see me on Tuesday nights and every other weekend. The attorney told me that the child support standard for the state of Minnesota for two children would be 34% of my gross earnings. I told him that I was making $280.00 a week. That's $1120.00 a month. My rent was $400.00, not including utilities. If I gave her $380.00 a month, that left $740.00. Less than the $400.00 for rent, I would have $340.00 left for food, gas, utilities, and my portion of the marital debt. I asked if there was any way that number could be negotiated. He told me that the Petitioner (Jessie) would have to sign a waiver and agree to a lesser amount. So, I told Jessie that if she would take $200.00 per month until I could get a job and earn more money, I would agree to everything else and not contest the divorce in any way. She agreed. I also asked her to take her maiden name back since she admitted that she didn't love me and wanted her independence.

She didn't want to do that. The day of the hearing came, and I couldn't bring myself to attend. I asked the attorney to inform the judge that I agreed to all the settlement terms and to call me when the hearing ended and it was final. He called at around 11:00 am that morning and told me the judge had signed it and he would record the final decree. I told him thank you, and I hung up the phone. I was distraught the rest of that day. I went from bouts of crying to sullen silence, staring out the window. I went outside for a walk and wandered around the city for a couple of hours, just trying to exhaust myself and use up the nervous energy coursing through my body. I was shaking so badly that I could not hold silverware to eat, and I struggled to swallow a glass of water. I decided to call my parents and come clean with everything I was going through. I needed to get away from Jessie and have a safe place to recover and start over. I also wasn't going to be able to afford to continue to live in Rochester. I called home, spoke with my mother, and asked if she and Dad would let me move home until I could find work and get myself back on my feet. They said yes. I was so grateful and finally had something to look forward to. I slept hard that night, and the next day, I called Jessie and told her I was moving back to Black River Falls. She was angry, thinking I should have consulted her before doing it. "How was that going to work with kids?" she inquired. I said I could still take them every other weekend, as agreed, but the Tuesday night visitation was off the table for now. She was pissed and wanted to know when she was going to get a night off? I said, "A night off from what?" "From having the kids," she said. I retorted that you're the one who told me that you were going to take the kids and leave if I didn't. I agreed to everything you wanted, and now you're pissed because you got it? I felt my anger starting to build and my voice raising in volume. I finally told her I was moving home, and she would have to deal with that. I called the apartment complex's landlord and told her I was leaving the next weekend. I would be moving out of state. I understood that I was breaking the lease and that she could keep my security deposit and seek damages for any rent due for the period of the lease. I said I would really appreciate it if she made every attempt to rent the apartment as soon as possible. She said that she would make an effort and expected that I might only be out another month's rent with the demand for apartments. I thanked her for her kindness and understanding. I loaded my Plymouth Horizon that weekend, took all my worldly belongings, and headed for Black River. I gave Jessie back the mattress, two chairs, silverware, linens, and towels. I said a tearful goodbye to the kids but told them that the next time we got together, they would be staying at Grandma and Grandpa's house with me. They kind of liked that idea. I said goodbye to Jessie, and she looked at me as if I had pissed on her new shoes. I, somehow, screwed her plan. The nice husband who would do anything she wanted was suddenly not following orders. Well, she wasn't done with me whether I knew it or not.

I arrived home and unloaded everything into my old bedroom. I was delighted to have my mother to talk to and have some company to take my mind off Jessie and the kids 24 hours a day. My dad was another story. He liked Jessie and was trying to figure out how I screwed it up. I tried not to talk to him about any of it and limited my exposure to him to meals and watching some westerns on TV at night.

I was still hurting inside and would leave the house as my anxiety would build and go for a ride in my car to shed a few tears and not have to listen to him lecture me on relationships and manhood. After the first week, Jessie called and wanted to make me aware that she had decided that she and the kids would move in with her boyfriend at his house just outside Pine Island, MN. Now I was the one whose shoes had been pissed on. I asked her again about her bullshit claim that she wanted her independence. I called her a liar and about a dozen less pleasant names. I also let her know that her new love better not does anything to hurt my kids, or I would not hesitate to come over there and break his fucking neck. I slammed the phone down and could feel the rage overtaking me like it had when I went after Jim Bradford.

I entered the basement and paced around, swearing under my breath. I was just so perplexed and hurt. How could she do it? What happened to the girl who needed me and snuck into my room the first night we stayed at the farm? I went back upstairs and into my room. Sitting on the edge of my bed, I had a flashback to prom night and the call from earlier. I was 18 years older and no closer to understanding. It would have been funny if I didn't feel unwanted, embarrassed, ashamed, and lost. I was tired of it. I had lost my ability to function anymore. I had no joy or nothing to look forward to in my life. I went out, climbed into my Horizon, and headed south down Hwy 27.

My mind raced, and all I could think about was how to make this stop. Then, a semi-truck came zipping past me, heading north toward Black River. It entered my mind that if he hit anything like a deer, that would end their life in a second for sure. Wait a minute. End their life in a second? Now, that sounded to me like a quick answer to my dilemma. This little Horizon was no match for a semi-truck at 60 mph.

I started practicing pulling into the oncoming traffic lane. How could I do it to make it look like an accident and not hurt whoever was driving the truck? I had to wait until the truck was close enough so the driver didn't have time to react. I wanted to avoid a near miss where I could be hurt badly and survive. I was near the Cataract and had practiced a few swerves. Here came another truck. I was getting ready to make the move, and for some reason, I glanced into the cab of the truck. Unexpectedly, I saw that it was a woman driving. I stayed in my lane. In my mind, I never intended to hurt a woman who might have kids. I slowed down as I entered Cataract and thought about returning home. I just kept driving with tears rolling down my face. Thankfully, I gave up on what I thought was my solution. I needed help, and going home seemed to offer no answer either. At that point, I just decided to keep driving and remembered what the doctor at St. Mary's had told me. If I needed to talk to someone, I should call her. I drove to St. Mary's in Rochester and entered the emergency room. I told them I had the feeling that I didn't want to live anymore and that I wanted to talk to my psychologist. I gave them her card, my hand shaking. I sat down in the waiting room, and within a few minutes, a nurse came with a wheelchair and took me upstairs to the mental health unit. My doctor met me there, and we had a brief discussion. She felt I should admit myself for treatment on a volunteer basis for at least 72 hours to give her time to give me the help I needed. I had no energy to do anything but agree to whatever she suggested. I spent ten days learning how to cope with my feelings. Right away, on the first night, they gave me a pill for anxiety that slowed my thoughts and allowed me to sleep. The doctor assured me that feeling out of control was normal, and she was sure the emotional trauma I had been through had caused a physical change in my brain. The emotional trauma, compounded by lack of sleep and inadequate nutrition, culminated in what she described as "clinical depression."

Without treatment, which would include individual and group therapy along with the medicine she prescribed, I would not have been able to recover on my own. I was in a battle for my soul. After I was settled in my room, I called my parents and let them know where I was. My mother was crying on the other end of the phone, and I told her I needed to do this and that I would be better when it was over.

After a couple of days, I slept better and regained my appetite. When they weighed me at the beginning of my stay, I was down to 172 lbs. My usual weight was around 210 to 217. No wonder my pants were falling. By the weekend, I was doing much better. I realized that I had a lot of pent-up feelings going way back to my childhood and my dad. He had no idea that his critical and demeaning parenting was affecting his children. He had the old-school mentality that you needed to toughen up your children so they could survive in the world. I had no clue that it affected me in the way that it did. I tried for years to do better and cover any hurt with effort or self-deprecating humor. I was longing to be loved for who I was. The desire to be loved by someone else was so great that I was willing to sacrifice myself. I learned I needed to love myself before I could honestly love someone else. It gave me a new focus on what was important in this life. The mistakes I had made were my fault and no one else. I made bad decisions sometimes, even for the right reasons. The floor nurse called me on Saturday and said I had a visitor. The counselors recommended that we think carefully before seeing anyone while in treatment. I asked the nurse if she knew who it was. She said that it was a lady who said her name was Jessie Eddy. What could she want, I wondered. I told the nurse I would talk to her in the visitation room. Jessie was in the room, and I walked in. First, she said, "Geez, aren't they feeding you here?" You are so skinny." I said, " Yes, they are feeding me just fine. What are you doing here?" She then told me that she wanted me to know that she and John were taking the kids up to a cabin on Lake of The Woods for a fishing trip and that they wouldn't be home if I wanted to call the kids. I started laughing. I just couldn't believe how oblivious she could be to my situation. "I'm in a mental health facility trying to deal with the loss of my wife and family to divorce and my wife having been unfaithful to me, and she wanted to do me a favor by telling me her new boyfriend was taking her and my kids on a fishing trip," I said. This was supposed to be a favor to me, so I wouldn't be inconvenienced if I tried to call them.

IN-FUCKING-CREDIBLE!

She looked at me, not sure what was happening. I shook my head and said, "Okay, thanks for letting me know. Have a good time, and tell the kids to call me when they get home." I turned and walked away. I heard her exit behind me. I knew from that moment on that I was over her.

A few days later, Jessie's mom and sister, Julie, came to see me at the hospital, and we had a good visit. They told me they loved me and would always consider me part of the family. I appreciated their kindness and told them I felt the same about them and the other kids. I even told them I felt sorry for Jessie because no one knew her better. I was sure she wouldn't be happy with anybody and no one would put up with her as I did. As it turned out, I was right. She would have a couple more relationships that went nowhere, and she is still alone.

A few days later, I called my parents, and they came over for a visit. My doctor thought it was vital for me to have a discussion with them about my treatment, what I had been through, and how we should talk about it going forward. My mom was so happy to see me, and I assured her I would be okay. My Dad, for the first time in my life, actually listened to what I had to say and expressed genuine concern that I was going to be okay as well. He even mentioned that he knew I was the most sensitive of all the kids, and he should have dealt with each of us as individuals and maybe not as harshly as he did. That was as close as he could ever get to an apology. I was healing, and it felt great. I promised never to allow myself to question my existence again. My past became my past, and it would stay there.

My new life started the day I left my treatment. Many things have happened in the 30 years since then.

The most important is that I have been "born again." I finally understood and listened to the voice of the Holy Spirit who Christ gave us. He spoke to me, and I wrote a letter of apology to Jessie for anything and everything I had ever said or done to hurt her. He also inspired this writing to testify to God's love for me. I share it only to make others know they are not alone in their desperate situation. *"In you, Lord, I have taken my refuge; let me never be put to shame; deliver me in your righteousness."* Psalm 31:1.